Fifty-four Devils

The Art & Folklore of Fortune-Telling with Playing Cards

By Cory Thomas Hutcheson,

Proprietor, New World Witchery

©2013 Cory Thomas Hutcheson

Contents

Overview   p. 5

     Red & Black   p. 8

     The Suits   p. 9

     Pips & Faces   p. 10

     Preparing to Read   p. 13

The Cards   p. 15

     Diamonds   p. 16

     Clubs   p. 19

     Hearts   p. 23

     Spades   p. 26

     The Jokers   p. 30

Table: The Cards & Their Meanings – A Quick Reference Guide   p. 33

The Spreads   p. 34

     One-Card   p. 36

     Three-Card   p. 37

     Five-Card (Full Spread)   p. 39

     Fifty-Four Card (Full Deck)   p. 45

Sample Card Spreads   p. 56

    One-Card   p. 57

    Three-Card   p. 59

    Five-Card (Full Spread)   p. 61

    Fifty-Four Card (Full Deck)   p. 68

Telling the Story   p. 72

    The Narrative of the Cards   p. 72

    Personal Note: Fairy Tales & Card Readings   p. 75

Final Notes   p. 78

Appendix: The Folklore of Cards   p. 79

Bibliography   p. 106

Overview

I have always been a fan of what's referred to as "a secret in plain sight." I love the idea that certain everyday objects have deeply a mystical significance which needs but the right pair of eyes to unveil it. Keys, coins, bottles, and boxes all find their way into my magical life and onto my household shelves, where most people ignore them. I, on the other hand, can turn to them at a moment's notice and use them as tools to open up the mysterious and wonderful world around me. So it is with playing cards.

In this small book, what I would like to do is explain my personal system of card divination, as well as some of the variants and influences which have shaped my practice. I'm not going to dive into an extensive history of playing cards or tarot cards, as those subjects are well-covered and well-documented in other sources. However, a little of the history that sometimes slips through the cracks (especially regarding playing cards) might be worth mentioning here.

While the absolute origin of pictographic cards is unknown, many believe they came out of India, China, or Turkey, possibly with the travelling Romany people (also frequently called "Gypsies"). An article from the 1895 *Journal of American Folklore* links these cards to "primitive arrows" and "emblems of the world quarters" and ties their origins to the Asian continent ("The Origin of Playing Cards," p. 250-51). By the 1500's, playing cards were very popular with the lower classes, and often cited as a vice by clerical and governmental documents throughout Europe—Charles Leland cites an Italian charm in which the cards are "twenty-five devils," reflecting the fiendish qualities imbued into a simple deck of printed paper (see "A Florentine Incantation..." in the Appendix). Playing cards remained intensely beloved, however, and appeared in the hands of some of the most elite members of European royalty and the courts attending them. Bohemian regent Rudolph I was reputed to have enjoyed playing cards, and Madame Lenormand became famous for her system of cards and card-reading during the reign of Napoleon. A copy of the *London Literary Gazette* from 1826 recounted this tale of Lenormand (spelled "Le Normand" in the article) and Empress Josephine:

> "The celebrated Mademoiselle Le Normand, who was so frequently consulted by the empress Josephine, and whom Napoleon himself did not totally disregard, was tried for witchcraft even a few years since; and it is surprising that the advocate who prosecuted her could seriously charge her with being familiar with spirits, and actually declare that she was able to raise demons and the dead. 'Josephine honoured her with her friendship, and bestowed upon her many marks of benevolence. After the return of Napoleon from the congress at Erfurt, the empress repeated to him, in the warmth of conversation, what Le Normand had announced to her some time before. The queen of Holland was present at the time. 'Ah !' said Napoleon, rubbing his hands, 'they pretend to penetrate into my designs, and consult the oracles: you must know, ladies, that I am not to be guessed at; to-morrow I will cause your prophetess to be arrested; and let me hear no more about her.' They attempted to appease him. 'It is useless,' said he; 'I shall give the orders immediately: I will not be imposed upon by a woman.' Josephine, who feared the effects of his indignation, sent at night privately Mademoiselle Aubert, one of her attendants, to acquaint Le Normand with his designs. Being informed of the emperor's determination, Le Normand, instead of being alarmed at the interruption of her tranquility, and regardless of the advice to attend to her own safety, said with the greatest *sang-froid* to Mademoiselle Aubert, that she felt obliged to the empress for her kindness,

but that she had nothing to fear from the emperor. This was reported to Josephine, who informed the emperor of Le Normand's reply...said Napoleon ; ...'I will allow her, however, to interfere with your affairs; but, with regard to mine, acquaint her that the least indiscretion shall cost her her liberty.' "

Cards have almost always been popular among the lower classes, too. Packs of cards came to America with settlers, sailors, and soldiers. In fact, in the late 1700's, a popular ballad, sometimes related as a folktale, called "The Soldier's Prayer-Book" described the suits, pips, and enumeration of playing cards in terms of biblical metaphor. For example, the fives represent the five wounds of Christ, the nines are the nine lepers healed by Jesus, and the tens are the Ten Commandments (see the Appendix "Folklore of Cards" for a complete reprint of the 1865 edition of this text). While this story may have been a white-wash for gambling soldiers eager to keep one of the few portable entertainments allowed them, it does register an important point: cards make wonderful tools for metaphoric interpretation.

So why playing cards instead of tarot cards? For one thing, playing cards of one kind or another have been more or less easily accessible since the 1600's, and are extremely versatile. The cards you play a game of blackjack with one day can be used to reveal the future the next. They also travel well in a pocket and are easily replaced if they get torn or damaged. Plantation owners in the antebellum South often thought little of slaves having decks of playing cards to amuse themselves in their few off hours (though in some places stricter masters prohibited them altogether). William Wells Brown, who provided a slave narrative for a character named "Uncle Frank," claimed that

7

each plantation also had at least one fortune-teller somewhere on the premises, and at least few of them used playing cards (Yronwode). Today, playing cards are an excellent way of divining even in plain sight. No one thinks much of two people over a table full of diamonds, spades, clubs, and hearts, while a Devil or Lovers card might raise eyebrows. Instead of Leland's twenty-five a reader can make his or her fifty-four devils dance as they reveal secrets and stories to the knowing eye.

My own system of playing card divination is largely based on the book *It's All in the Cards*, by Chita Lawrence, and the rhyme "For the Witch of Poor Memory" by Dawn R. Jackson, with a significant amount of additional material I've picked up from other books, teachers, and experiences over time. What I outline here will be *my own* understanding of these cards, so please do not take it as gospel, and find or refine a method that works for you.

Red & Black

Like most people who practice cartomancy, I break the major meanings of the cards down by color and suits. However, unlike a lot of other practitioners, I don't ascribe these suits to tarot parallels or elemental attributes. There are some connections, of course, as hearts and cups both signal emotion-based interpretations, but it's not an absolute or indelible link.

First, **black cards indicate "negative" or "no" answers**, while **red cards are "positive" or "yes"** answers. This is most important in short readings, which I'll address a little later. Some will say that having more black cards than red is a sign of negativity, but honestly, the only truly "negative" cards in an extended reading are the spades, in my opinion.

Getting hung up on the red vs. black significance can short circuit a reading, too. While it is helpful in a way to be able to "summarize" the reading based on the proportion of "positive" red cards to "negative" black ones, it might also predispose you as a reader to offer a particularly strong interpretation as you continue with the session. Seeing lots of red cards may make you think "Oh, a very pleasant reading! Good news for the client!" but when you see that, in fact, you've actually got a Seven of Diamonds and an Ace and Seven of Hearts in your reading, there are distinct possibilities for a negative reading that you might ignore based on your positive bias (that may all be quite confusing now, but as you get through the book it should become clearer).

Basically, as always with divinatory methods, keep an open mind. **Use the colors of the cards as a loose guide**, but don't get invested in them before thinking about the individual card meanings.

The Suits

If you've had any experience with tarot, understanding the different meanings for each suit might be easier. Then again, it might be harder, as many tarot readers have preset notions about suit correspondences. I advise that a reader spend time with the cards and determine what patterns emerge from continual use. But I will definitely admit that having at least a rough concept of what each suit means can be incredibly helpful. For me, I look at the suits in the following way:

9

Hearts – Family, friends, love, and lovers. Also emotions and things which are deeply felt.

Clubs – Work and business. One's "calling" or destiny. Also conflict, discussion, and debate.

Diamonds – Money, luck, fortune, happiness. Also news, letters, and socializing.

Spades – Tears, suffering, woe. War, fighting, violence. Also change, warning, and doubts/fears.

I'll get into each of these suits a little more when I break down the individual cards, but this should give you some idea what I see when I do a layout for a reading. If I see lots of diamonds and clubs, I know that someone's done some good work he or she will be well compensated for coming around the bend. All hearts means that the client is emotionally invested in the reading, or that he or she is dealing with deep family or friendship questions. Spades and clubs together would be a sign that the client's job might be in jeopardy, or that work is very unfulfilling for him or her.

Next, we'll get into the significance of the pips on the cards, but it is good to keep the overall meanings of the suits in mind as we go forward.

Pips and Faces

There are lots of different systems of interpreting the card numbers and the royals. Some are fairly simplistic (mine definitely are) and some get incredibly detailed, looking at astrological and numerological significance in cabbalistic and ceremonial magical contexts. I'm not a particularly good ceremonialist, so I tend to use a fairly straightforward system focusing on key concepts associated with each number. I can probably demonstrate better than I can explain, so here's my numbering system.

Aces – Beginnings; Primary or Solitary things
Twos – Pairs; Couples; Exchange
Threes – Growth; Wishes
Fours – Decisions; Stagnation; Choices
Fives – Groups; Bodily things; Gains/Losses
Six – Paths
Sevens – Epitome cards*; Inversions; Trouble
Eights – Talking; Ideas
Nines – Patience; Ambition; Expansion
Tens – Completion; Endings
Jacks – Youth; Children; Messages; Peers
Queens – Women or a particular woman; Beauty; Mothers;
      Nurses; Teachers
Kings – Men or a particular man; Wisdom; Age; Power; Judges

> *A note on "epitome" cards – the Sevens of each suit represent the most concentrated form of that suit. Often, there's a somewhat negative connotation to this intensity. Yet, this does not necessarily mean all good or all bad. For example, the seven of spades can mean "tears" as an epitome card, but if those tears are near lots of red cards, they are likely tears of joy.

The number combinations can also lead to a certain amount of interpretation. For instance, if you had several threes and nines, that would guide you towards a reading about opportunities and very quick growth (because both cards are about growth/expansion). A seven, five, and four might indicate bad choices and losses that come out of those choices. A king with a six might mean a teacher or elder is going to help guide the questioner in a new direction.

Royal cards (or "face cards") also have a certain potency that the numeric cards lack. I sometimes include aces as a face card, but this really depends on the reading and the number of other face cards around it. It's sort of like spiritual blackjack—it can be the highest or lowest value depending on the other cards. The other face cards usually represent particular people or major events in the subject's life. Getting a king and a queen of the same suit can often indicate "parents" or the parental guidance which shaped the questioner's life. You'll see more about these as we explore them in depth later on, but for now just know that royals, aces, and sevens all mean "pay attention to this reading." There are some divinatory systems (such as the card-reading taught in some branches of *curanderismo*) which also remove the queens from the deck before reading. This dates back to a European practice based on a specific deck, but don't be surprised if you don't see them in someone's reading. As a final word on royals, there are two special royals in my system of divination: the King and Queen of Hearts. Depending on the gender of the client, one of these cards will represent him or her (the king for a man, the queen for a woman). We'll look at how that works later on, though. All of these interpretations are also deeply linked to the suits, of course, and to where they fall during the reading.

Knowing the cards intimately will always help any reader, but I feel it is equally important to get one's head right before beginning a cartomancy session. To that end, I will here give a brief glimpse into my preparatory methods for any card reading.

Preparing to Read

Because reading cards is a form of divination, I feel it has a spiritual component. I know many people do not feel this way, and instead see the cards as psychological tools. If that description fits you and the card readings work without any spiritual connections for you, then please feel free to skip this section. If, on the other hand, you do feel that divination proceeds from something other than the unconscious—be it a divine source, helpful spirits, astrological attunements, or any other influential force—then you may be interested in the fairly simple methods I use to prepare for a reading.

Among Afro-Caribbean traditions like Palo Mayombe, oracular systems like the *dilogun* are prayed over before use. Similarly, I use a set of very simple prayers before beginning any card reading (spoken while shuffling the cards):

1. Psalm 23 – "The Lord is My Shepherd..."
2. The Lord's Prayer
3. Ave Maria/Hail Mary
4. A final prayer asking for the direction of my ancestors, guardian spirits, and guides on the other side

My particular prayers reflect two things: 1) my Catholic upbringing, and 2) an inherent laziness when it comes to changing what works. I have some very deep spiritual convictions, most of which do not sit comfortably within any orthodox Judeo-Christian religious system. Yet I rely on prayers from that tradition simply because I know they work for me. If you were so inclined, a reading of any prayer that fits comfortably within your own practices would likely be just as effective. A Buddhist *sutra* or an incantation from the Egyptian

Book of the Dead could invite the spiritual frame of mind and the attention of otherworldly forces appropriate to your efforts. If you are working from a more broadly Pagan or neo-Pagan tradition, I would highly recommend *The Pagan Ritual Prayer Book*, by Ceisiwr Smith for its lyrical and thoughtful prayers.

The first three prayers I listed can all be easily found in any number of sources, so I will not bother to repeat them here. The final prayer to my personal spiritual companions is personal, but I would like to give you some flavor of that kind of evocation, so I will here give a somewhat generic version of that portion of the preparation:

> *Ancestors, blessed Saints, guardians, & guides –*
> *Please bless this tool of divination.*
> *Bless it that it might open doors into insight.*
> *Bless my hands as they turn the cards,*
> *That they may always find what you will them to find.*
> *Bless my eyes as they read the cards,*
> *That they may always see the meanings you reveal.*
> *Bless my ears, that they may hear your guiding words.*
> *Bless my lips, that I speak your meanings clearly.*
> *Bless my mind and heart, that they remain open,*
> *Open to receiving your wisdom through this simple tool.*
> *Amen.*

If you don't work with Saints, or guardian spirits, or ancestors (and why don't you? They're lovely people!), I imagine you could adjust this sort of prayer to fit other spiritual systems as well. My primary purpose in sharing this information is to simply say that this sort of work requires a receptive mental and spiritual state, and that those states are fairly easily facilitated by a few moments of meditative prayer before reading.

With that being said, I would also like to say I do not necessarily do this same course of prayer immediately before *every* reading. If I am doing several readings in a row, a single set of incantations prior to beginning is sufficient for me. Should I interrupt my work at the cards for any significant period of time—sleep, food, or good conversation with friends—then I would repeat my preparations when I next sit down to shuffle the deck. Again, this is essentially about creating headspace which is conducive to card reading, so if you still feel "tuned in," as it were, you likely can forgo a full repetition of prayers (although you might perhaps just mutter a word or two under your breath to be sure).

Now, on to the individual cards.

The Cards

Now we're going to look at individual cards and their significance in my readings. I'll basically tell you a few key words, and then elaborate a bit on potential interpretations of these cards. Most of my system comes out of years of practice using playing cards for divination, as well as for games. I have found that in some cases, my personal work with a particular card has shown me a meaning different from the one I originally learned. When it comes to these sorts of fortune-telling methods, practice makes perfect. Think of these symbols as hallmarks of a particular 'spirit' (or devil, if you like), and the cards as individual beings. You might be surprised by what they can do, if you let them lead you.

15

Now, the cards! Let's start with:

Diamonds

Remember that diamonds in general signify money, fortune, luck, and happiness. They also can relate to messages or news, or social interaction.

Ace – A letter; A coin. The Ace of Diamonds indicates some new money or new information entering the questioner's life. It can also have to do with a sudden shift in luck—if preceded and followed by spades, that could mean bad luck. Additionally, due to the solitary nature of the pip, it could mean being very careful with your news, luck, or money—keeping it to yourself, as it were.

Two – Birds (as in "a little birdie told me"); Exchange of funds. This card is about sharing, whether that's news and gossip (like the birds), or sharing your luck or fortune with someone else. It *can* indicate a partnership of some kind, but usually not a business one so much as a financial one. For example, if it were paired with a card connected to a friend or lover, you might be moving in with that person soon (because you'll be yoking yourself to them financially).

Three – Gifts; A fountain. The Three of Diamonds shows generosity—sometimes even unwilling generosity. Someone who draws this card likely "throws his/her money away," just like one throws pennies in a fountain (if you're singing "Three Coins in a Fountain" right now, I sympathize with you). This may seem like a sign of irresponsibility, but it can also mean *receiving* a gift, or an expansion of fortunes which allows the person to be generous.

Four – The purse/money bag; No news. With the Four of Diamonds, the reader will need to figure out if the reading is about money or information, as it changes the card's meaning a bit. If the question is financial, the four indicates a stable monetary situation, but also one without any chance of growing—much like a closed purse neither receives nor spends money. In the case of information, this card indicates a dull waiting period, possibly a prolonged one. This can mean "no news is good news," or that the client must wait on tenterhooks for a proper resolution to his/her situation.

Five – Good luck; Laughter. This card shows the subject surrounded by friends, fortune, and happiness. It's not the all-encompassing joy found in other cards like the Ten of Diamonds but it's generally positive nonetheless. Depending on context, however, it can also mean something like "the last laugh," and have slightly more sinister connotations.

Six – Streets of Gold; Good decisions. No, not the Yellow Brick Road, but the idea's the same. The client's on the right path and merely needs to continue doing what he/she is doing and success will come. Paired with a card like an Ace, this card may mean recent decisions have been good; paired with a King or a Queen the client is probably getting very good advice from someone.

Seven – Lies; Deceit and falsehood. The Seven of Diamonds indicates that the questioner is being lied to by someone. This lie may or may not have to do with money, but almost always has to do with happiness. Perhaps the client is happy being lied to, and little white lies sustain him/her—this could certainly be the case if a Jack of Diamonds, Clubs, or Hearts were nearby. More often, though, the lies indicate trouble to come.

Eight – Gossip; Idle chatter. Much like the Two of Diamonds, this card means an exchange of information, although it usually is information of little value. It can also indicate talking about money, getting good news about one's fortunes or finances, or someone's natural wit. Paired with something like the Two of Spades, it might mean something like "loose lips sink ships," and that one should hold one's tongue for a while.

Nine – Daydreams; Peace and contentment. Think of this card as a leisurely day spent in the sun with nothing particular to do. It's a card of relative idleness, but without any real negativity. It's a well-earned rest, a chance to plan for the future, and time to stop and smell the flowers. Beware, though, if it's paired with a four of any kind, as it may mean that all one's plans are but pipe dreams, destined to disappear like clouds in an afternoon sky. Or something like that.

Ten – A treasure chest; Sunlight; Joy. With the Ten of Diamonds, the client can expect great happiness. In the context of other good luck cards, this may mean an unexpected windfall or a sudden improvement in circumstances. The Ten of Diamonds leaves little room for any sorrow or woe, and generally indicates the fulfillment of financial goals and personal dreams. Of course, as Willy Wonka said, "Do you know what happened to the boy who suddenly got everything he ever wanted?" Oh, wait, he lived happily ever after...

Jack – Good news; A girl. This card displays a young boy (or possibly a young girl, hence the card's alternate meaning). At one time these cards were known as Knaves instead of Jacks, and would have been similar to a knight's squire. In the context of a card reading, this Jack means that some good news is about to arrive. Or that a beautiful girl is about to arrive. Which might also be good news, depending on your point of view.

Queen – The good wife; A wedding; Sensuality. This Queen is all about duty and splendor. She could be a mother or wife in the questioner's life who inspires joy and happiness, or provides sound financial advice. More likely, though, she indicates someone who does what must be done or a woman with a deeply sexual side. She can also mean a wedding (and thus a large expense and a large celebration), or in some cases a big party (for instance if she appeared alongside "friend" cards like the Queen or Jack of Clubs).

King – A bank; A civil trial; Wisdom with money. The King of Diamonds means power through money or fortune. Pulled with several spades, the client can expect to face some financial trials (literally in a courtroom or possibly only figuratively). Alternately, pulled with clubs or diamonds, this card probably means that money is being invested wisely, or that there is a man in the questioner's life who provides very good advice when it comes to luck and money.

Clubs

Clubs are work, destiny, plans and debate. Remember that as you do your readings.

Ace – A cave; Solitary contemplation. This card tells the reader that the subject should take some time to really evaluate his or her life. Has he/she got goals? Is he/she working to reach them, or should there be some reevaluation of priorities? This is a lonely card, but not necessarily a bad one—often we need moments of intense personal reflection before we can move on to do the great things we are capable of.

Two – A handshake; Business partnership. The Two of Clubs shows an agreement or arrangement made between two people, often for the sake of business or stability. It can indicate a treaty or alliance of some kind, or a pairing up to overcome obstacles in the way. Pulled with something like a Two of Spades, it may mean the impending end of a previous business partnership.

Three – A stone wall; Obstacles. In most cases, threes indicate wishes or growth, so this card may seem odd. However, the setbacks provided by a good obstacle also provide the impetus to overcome them oftentimes. Usually this card means that whatever challenges the subject faces, whether they be business troubles or a lack of personal direction, he/she can and will overcome them. Paired with something like a Three of Hearts or Diamonds, such progress is likely just around the bend.

Four – A horse and cart; A plowed field. This card is about potential. The Four of Clubs definitely means that for the moment nothing is happening, but that now is the time to prepare for inevitable change. By "tilling" and "plowing" oneself or one's business plans, the eventual outcome will be far better than one would get just sitting on one's hands. If this card appears with a Nine of Clubs, that outcome is ripe and should show up very soon.

Five – A barn; A healthy body. The Five of Clubs is encouraging. It can represent either a full barn (which in turn stands for abundance and hard work paying off) or a strong, healthy body. If this card were at the end of a reading full of cards which indicated illness (such as a Five or Nine of Spades), a recovery should be expected. An inversion of that order might mean deteriorating health, however, so context is important.

Six – Footprints; A clear trail. A person who gets this card in his/her reading probably has a definitive sense of purpose, or has recently begun some activity that he/she finds very fulfilling. This can be a career, a hobby, or even a friendship of some kind. If the appropriate King or Queen of Hearts comes after this card, it might be a sign that true love ("wuv…twue wuv") is on the horizon.

Seven - Doubts/Worries. The Seven of Clubs indicates that the client is very troubled by something. So troubled, in fact, that it is likely hindering or debilitating the questioner in some way. Paired with something like the Seven of Spades and/or the Ace of Clubs, he/she likely spends a lot of time alone and crying over something that he/she feels powerless to change. The nice thing about this card (and there is a nice thing) is that for the most part, all the troubles are really in the asker's head. They can be overcome, but it may take a mental sea change to effect that change.

Eight - Shop talk; A table or bench. When the work day finishes, it's nice to crowd around a table with friends, family, and sometimes even co-workers for a drink or a meal. Often the events of the day get rehashed, with details added or subtracted as conversation directs. That's what this card is all about. It shows people getting together to share the tricks of their particular trades, make plans for times ahead, or even occasionally plumb the mysteries of the universe, depending on how much beer is at the table.

Nine - Reaping; A forest. The Nine of Clubs shows things that have grown and how we deal with them as human beings. In some cases, we reap what we've sown and prepare for hard times ahead hoping that what we have will be enough. Sometimes, we wander through the trees getting lost, hoping we'll find our way back again. A questioner finding this card may be having trouble making sense of his or her life, but there is still plenty of hope left. Followed by something like a Ten of Hearts or Clubs, this card simply means that a dark night soon reveals a bright dawn.

Ten - A herd or flock; Clouds. This card is abundance, completion, and satisfaction. It is definitely all about rewards, comfort, and a job well done. It completes the sense of accomplishment found in the Five of Clubs, and adds the element of restfulness. The seeker's found his or her calling, home life is happy and stable, and/or business is steady and fulfilling. The clouds, heavy with rain on the horizon, are pouring down copiously. This is the "pat on the back" or "Miller time" card.

Jack – A friend; A sibling. The Jack of Clubs is a peer, whether that's a co-worker, a good friend, or a sibling. This is someone with whom the questioner has a mutual respect. The Jack can also indicate business news of some kind (especially if an Ace or Two of Diamonds or an Eight of Clubs shows up), and may also indicate a young boy entering the client's life.

Queen – A mother; A nurse; A wise woman. This is a card indicating someone very smart, very strong, and very helpful. The seeker probably knows exactly who this card represents when he/she sees it, and also probably knows exactly what kind of advice this person would give (think of this as a conscience card). This card can also mean a mother hen, too, though likely only if connected to an argumentative card, like the Eight of Spades. Conflict in the Clubs is productive, however, so even a mother hen has her place. Finally, this card indicates nurturing. Paired with something like an Ace of Clubs, it likely means taking the time to heal old emotional wounds before moving forward with something or someone new.

King – A father; A judge; A general. The King of Clubs is someone with authority, someone who can give an order and get things done. He may not always be nice about it, but he has his reasons for driving people so hard. This person is someone wise, though perhaps also someone very stubborn and set in his ways. For those who have issues with feeling judged all the time, this card could be troubling, but it may also mean that the questioner must face his or her fears and forge ahead. This is a card about what *must* be done, and living up to expectations.

Hearts

This suit has to do with deep emotions as well as family, friends, and lovers. These cards often represent people well-known to the questioner.

Ace – A kiss; A new romance; Feeling lonely. Pulling the Ace of Hearts in a reading means that likely a new lover has entered the picture, or at the very least a formerly bland relationship has taken on new life. Generally it's a positive card, but next to something like a Two of Spades it can mean a period of separation and loneliness.

Two – Lovers; Coupling; The sex card. This is the card that inspires knowing smiles and lecherous grins. Simply put, it's about sex. Not so simply put, it can also be about and deeply emotionally intimate connection with someone else, including a family member (try not to mix those two meanings together). So if you pulled it with say the King or Queen of Clubs, it likely means a family relationship, while a lay next to any Jack might mean a delightful tryst.

Three – A wish granted; A full cup. The Three of Hearts means that something deeply longed for is about to appear. This isn't quite the fulfillment found with the Ten of Diamonds or the Ten of Hearts, but it does generally mean at least one thing will go right.

Four – A trunk or travel case; A lock. Like with other fours, this card shows a relative stagnation. However, in the case of the Four of Hearts, that could also mean incubation or preparation. The image of a hope chest or a steamer trunk fits this card, with all their promised potential for excitement, romance, marriage, and just life in general. However, getting mired down in preparation can lead to a life of lockdown, where everything is being kept just so, and never given the opportunity for use.

Five – A chapel; Fertility; A bed. The Five of Hearts shows the healthy development of a romance, leading to family and (potentially) marriage. Paired with something like the Queen of Diamonds, it almost certainly means a wedding of some kind. Paired with a Jack of Hearts, be prepared for a new member of the family in nine months. Paired with a Nine of Clubs, however, this card could just mean someone needs a good night's sleep.

Six – A dog; Loyalty and stamina; Long-term relationships. If the questioner gets the Six of Hearts in a reading, he or she can expect to be in it for the long haul, whatever "it" may be. It could be a family situation, a romance, or even—if paired with something like the Two of Spades—a lengthy divorce. However, the upside to this card is its dog imagery. Paired with a lover card like the Two of Hearts, it indicates a sincere and faithful mate, one who loves unconditionally and who will always be there.

Seven – Hate; Fear. This card shows a love that has grown too strong and become hate, or possibly fear and terror of another person. If the reader sees this card with something like the Five or Nine of Spades, it's a sign that the relationship will end in violence and help should be sought immediately. Alternatively, with something like the Ace of Clubs, this may indicate self-loathing which needs be overcome. It's also possible that the Seven of Hearts will act as a warning in a reading, alerting the subject to the presence of an enemy.

Eight – Flirtation; Pillow talk. While the Two of Hearts is all about doing it, this card is all about *talking* about doing it. The Eight of Hearts shows that giddy, fun stage of flirtation and wooing that so often appears early in the relationship. It can also mean a sweet, tender intimacy and connecting with a partner on an emotional as well as physical level.

Nine – A little house/cottage; A new life. When a client pulls this card, it usually has to do with the establishment of a new family or a new home. Paired with something like the Four of Hearts or Five of Clubs, it may mean saving for a new house, or possibly moving away. If aces show up, however, pay attention to them, as they may indicate a sudden shift in life circumstances which leads to a new life that the client doesn't actually want.

Ten – A happy family; A fire. With the Ten of Hearts, everything about one's emotional and personal life seems to be falling into place. Romances go well, family relationships are strong, and everything's good. Think of being gathered around a nice warm fire with friends and family, enjoying a perfect summer evening. Be aware, however, that as with all fires, this one can burn. Paired with an Ace of Spades, be prepared for an upheaval in happiness.

Jack – A baby; A cradle; A young boy. This card is one that makes plenty of clients nervous, and some extremely happy. Because of its strong associations with a newborn child, the Jack of Hearts often tells of a pregnancy, especially when matched to something like the Five of Hearts. This card can also have to do with calm and peace, though, even indicating a period of self-pampering in a way. In some cases, the card simply refers to a boy or young man in the client's life.

Queen – The client; Soulmate. Remember how I said the King and Queen of Hearts were unusual? That's because they are used to represent the actual client in a reading. If a reader has a female client, she is represented by the Queen of Hearts. If the reader's client is male, this card represents that perfect, ideal lover or soulmate. One of these two cards, at least, will always show up in every extended reading (more on that when we talk about layouts). The presence of both indicates a preexisting marriage or a deep and abiding love.

King – The client; Soulmate. Just like the Queen of Hearts, this card can represent either a male client or a soulmate. I know some people will ask about homosexual couples, and I will say that despite the gender pairings implied by the card faces, the meaning "soulmate" still applies to gay couples. Since there aren't two Kings of Hearts in a deck, a gay man will see his ideal mate represented as a Queen of Hearts. The reverse is true if a gay woman sees a King of Hearts in her reading—she can expect to meet the girl of her dreams.

Spades

These are the cards of woe, suffering, and fighting. Consider them warnings or signs of trouble that may yet be avoided.

Ace – Death; Sudden change. This card is paralleled by the Death card in the tarot deck. And like its counterpart, it doesn't necessarily mean physical death, but instead a sudden transformation or an ending. Much of this card's meaning depends upon what it's next to. If it is with a Six of Clubs, it might mean that a business venture will come to an abrupt termination. With Threes from Diamonds and/or Hearts, the client can stop expecting others to give them anything...they are on their own. This card can also indicate deep isolation, and in some cases might even mean a period of contemplation, but again, it depends on context.

Two – A duel; A separation. The Two of Spades means that someone is itching for a fight, and there's a good chance they'll get one. Paired with cards like the Two or Nine of Hearts, a romantic separation is imminent. If it sits next to a personal card, like a jack, king, or queen, it's likely there will be a falling out with that person soon.

Three – A battle; Setbacks and obstacles. Unlike the obstacles presented by the Three of Clubs, the roadblocks that come out of this card are not about developing oneself and overcoming difficult trials. Instead, this card is about fighting through the hardest parts and living to see another day. Metaphorically, the Three of Spades might indicate a bitter falling out with one's parents (if next to a King or Queen of clubs) or a difficult economic situation at one's job (with a Six of Diamonds or Clubs).

Four – The Four Horsemen; A mire. Seeing a four in any suit indicates feeling a little stuck, but seeing a Four of Spades means being immobilized. It can also presage illness, poverty, violence, or even death. It means that if the subject doesn't make some changes—difficult as they may be to make—there could be some dire consequences. However, there are positive ways to see this card. If it is followed, for example, by the Five and Jack of Hearts, it may mean that someone who's been trying to get pregnant will soon be able to, though it won't be easy. Overall, though, consider this a definite "warning" card.

Five – Illness; A corpse. This suit is just full of jolly things, isn't it? The Five of Spades indicates sickness, disease, pain, etc. It can also mean that there's something that needs to be buried, like a hatchet between the client and someone he/she is feuding with. Paired with cards like the other Fives or the Ten of Clubs, it generally means that the client will beat the illness or deal with the skeletons in his/her closet. With a Nine or Ten of Spades, however, things get worse.

Six – A devil; Temptation; Bad decisions. If the Queen of Clubs is the angel on your shoulder, the Six of Spades is on the other side with red pajamas and a pitchfork. The nice thing about this card is that any temptations it brings up can be recognized and dealt with. But sometimes it's fun to give into temptation, too, so pay attention to the other cards. If you see lots of red cards around this card, it may mean a little harmless vice. With a Two of Hearts and a Five of Spades, however, it may mean that a sexual relationship is becoming destructive.

Seven – Tears; Blood; War. I've already mentioned that the tears implied by the Seven of Spades can be tears of sorrow or tears of joy, depending on context. This card may also be a warning that violence is not far away, or that something deep down inside the subject is affected by the overall reading. But the sevens always carry a twist. While the sevens of the other suits tend to have some potent negativity, the Seven of Spades can have a very good side. It can imply a great deal of strength, mastery of a situation, or even coming victory and glory. Caution is always best, though. If this card lands with the Ace, Five, Nine, or Ten of Spades, heads will roll (or have already).

Eight – An argument; Shouting. Communication is important, but how a person communicates is also vital. Pulling the Eight of Spades means that the client is not making him/herself clear and likely finds him/herself constantly embattled and unable to resolve the problems in his/her life. It can also mean long-standing arguments with those close to the client. If it were with a Queen of Clubs and a Five of Hearts, it could be a mother-in-law, for example.

Nine – A funeral; A coffin; A ghost. The Nine of Spades looks like a funeral procession as scene from above, with pallbearers carrying a black coffin (at least that's one way to see it). This could indicate some kind of grieving process, the need for ritual and order to restore balance, or just a need to put an end to things. In some cases, this card may mean that someone or something from the past is still haunting the subject (it may even indicate a literal haunting). Matched with something like the

Jack of Clubs or Jack of Hearts, it might mean an old friend or an old flame of some kind.

Ten – A cemetery; A ruined church. This card shows the aftermath of woe and trouble, and in that way it's actually not all that bad. It shows that the worst is over, and that all that's left is to pick up the pieces and move on. It can also be a peaceful card, a return to calm and quiet, or even to innocence in a way. Paired with a card like the Six of Clubs, it might mean a lapse in faith and a need to reevaluate one's beliefs about something.

Jack – A rebel; Bad news; A backstabber. The Jack of Spades is a bad boy/girl, someone not to be trusted but who likely is very seductive and enticing. With a card like the Six of Spades beside it, it might mean the kind of lover who is no good, but incredibly desirable. With a Two or Eight of Diamonds, it means that gossip and slander are spreading about the client, and steps should be taken to staunch it. The Jack of Spades can also simply mean bad news is on the horizon, so be prepared for it.

Queen – A cruel mother; A seductress; Jealousy; A female rival. With this particular queen, watch out! She's intensely powerful and knows how to use that power to get what she wants. She is trying to take something from the subject, be it a lover, money, or happiness in general. However, this card can also be a warning that the subject is becoming too jealous for no reason, which is almost an opposite reading in a way. So again context is important. Paired with a Six of Spades or an Eight of Hearts, it's likely this woman is trying to wreck a relationship. Paired with a Six of Hearts, though, it probably means that the subject is needlessly jealous.

King – A criminal; An executioner; Wrath; A male rival. The King of Spades is powerful, too, and just as vicious as his queen.

He is not the just judge found in the clubs, but an executioner ready to exact a penalty for any wrongdoings. He will take what is rightfully the client's if he can, or attack when the client is the weakest. If this card appears, the client should attempt to make amends for any transgressions, and turn to friends or family for support in case hard times lie ahead.

The Jokers

In most standard card decks, you will have two Joker cards. Frequently these are simply design cards with some signature item from the deck manufacturer, which might be incorporated into a game as a "wild card" at some point. Do they have significance for a reader? In many cases, people remove the Jokers, as they don't seem to have much to say. Removing cards is all well and good—in fact the Spanish method of cartomancy calls for the removal of Queens from the deck—but I have learned that for my readings, the Jokers actually can serve a strong purpose.

When I do readings, a Joker popping up means that some aspect of the question actively *wants* to stay hidden. The Jokers bring an air of mystery to the layout, indicating that something must remain unknown for the time being. Frequently, Jokers pop up in positions to do with the future—I don't think I've ever actually had them pop up in any other location during a reading—and tell the reader and subject that the universe has some surprises in store. No fair rattling the package, so to speak, as you'll just have to wait until it's time to find out what's brewing.

I do sometimes circumvent the Joker's mysterious presence by pulling another card to "signify" on it, but the meaning usually has nothing to do with the pip on the card. At best, the suit will give you an indication what area of the person's life will hold the secret to that which has been hidden—a Club card might signify that a surprise at work is coming (we hope it is a good one!). A court card like a Queen or King could indicate that a new person will be entering the picture, but that sometimes can be misleading. Above all, the Joker indicates that the universe has a sense of humor, so even if you spend an inordinate amount of time guessing just what the Joker means, the cosmos will likely give you an outcome that defies all expectations yet fits within the context of the reading. For the most part, it is wise to respect the jolly fool hiding in your deck and accept the mystery he brings to the reading.

If you do choose to remove the Jokers when you read, that is completely sensible. After all, we read cards to add insight and shed light on our questions, not to receive cryptic messages about obscured events. The best way to approach the Joker is to try reading with and without him a few times, and see what works best.

Table: The Cards & Their Meanings – A Quick Reference Guide

For those who want to be able to put this system into practice but who have trouble memorizing the specific meanings, I thought it might be helpful to include this little table. It gives keyword interpretations for each of the cards based on the meanings I described above. You could copy or print this page and keep it folded up with your favorite deck of cards so that you're always ready to read at a moment's notice. Or, if you don't carry a deck with you constantly (why don't you?!?), you could simply make a little wallet card or insert out of this page instead and take it with you in case you happen to be someplace with both an eager client and a random deck of cards (because you're horribly unprepared and don't carry cards with you, you see).

	♦	♣	♥	♠
A	Letter/Coin	Cave/ Solitude	Kiss/ New Romance/ Feeling Lonely	Death/ Sudden Change
2	Bird/Exchange of Funds	Handshake/ Business Partnership	Lovers/ Coupling/ Sex	Duel/ Separation
3	Gifts/Fountain	Stone Wall/ Obstacles	Wish Granted/ Full Cup	Battle/ Setbacks
4	Purse/No News	Horse & Cart/ Plowed Field	Trunk or Travel Case/ Lock	Four Horsemen/ Mire
5	Good Luck/Laughter	Barn/ Healthy Body	Chapel/ Fertility/ Bed	Illness/ Corpse
6	Streets of Gold/Good Decisions	Footprints/ Clear Trail	Dog/ Loyalty/ Stamina	Devil/ Temptation/ Bad Decisions
7	Lies/Deceit	Doubts/ Worries	Hate/Fear	Tears/Blood/ War
8	Gossip/Idle Chatter	Shop Talk/ Table or Bench	Flirtation/ Pillow Talk	Argument/ Shouting
9	Daydreams/ Peace	Reaping/ Forest	Little House/ Cottage/ New Life	Funeral/ Coffin/ Ghost
10	Treasure Chest/ Sunlight/Joy	Herd or Flock/ Clouds	Happy Family/ Fire	Cemetery/ Ruined Church
J	Good News/ Girl	Friend/ Sibling	Baby/ Cradle/ Young Boy	Rebel/ Bad News/ Backstabber
Q	Good Wife/ Wedding/ Sensuality	Mother/ Nurse/ Wise Woman	Client/ Soulmate	Cruel Mother/ Seductress/ Jealousy/ Female Rival
K	Bank/Civil Trial/ Wisdom with Money	Father/ Judge/ General	Client/ Soulmate	Criminal/ Executioner/ Wrath/ Male Rival
JOKER	Mystery	Hidden Meanings	A Secret	Sense of Humor

Table: The Cards & Their Meanings

The Spreads

In the system I work with, spreads tend to be very simplistic. Only a small number of cards are used to provide divination, and the overall structure of the reading will be guided mostly by the completed spread taken as a whole. There are many cartomancy systems which use more cards and which take longer to do (the most elaborate reading I regularly do takes about 30-45 minutes at most), but anytime I've attempted anything bigger than the methods I'm about to demonstrate, I've felt the answers were too vague to be of any use. That is just me, however, and others may find tremendous success with those expanded readings.

Basically, there are a few different readings you can do:
- A one-card yes/no reading
- A three card time-based spread (past/present/future, morning/noon/night, etc.)
- An extended "five-card" spread (though this is a bit of a misnomer, as you'll see in a moment)
- A protracted, highly-involved fifty-four card spread (a "full deck" one, as it were)

I'm sure other people have other methods, but these are the ones I work with so I'll be explaining from my point of view only.

Before you do any spread, contact Spirit(s) if you like. If you don't know how to do that or don't feel like that will help your reading, you can bypass this step, but if you do have any experience with necromantic work you'll know that it aids divination tremendously (see "Preparing to Read" earlier in the book for guidance). In some of the illustrations below, you'll be seeing candles and a skull in the picture. While these *are* a part of *my* Ancestral contact work, I'd like to be up front in saying they are in these pictures more for show than anything else. I do sometimes contact Ancestors via the cards (mostly because my cards are handed down from my mother, so if I want to speak to her they're a great medium for that), but generally speaking I don't have a lot of paraphernalia during a cartomancy session. Part of the charm of reading with playing cards is their ubiquitous and unassuming nature, so getting all the trappings and trimmings of a full Ancestor contact working out is a bit overkill. But it looks nice in pictures.

Often, a short prayer to the effect of "Spirit(s), guide my hands as I shuffle these cards, my eyes as I read them, and my mind as I speak their meaning" will suffice. A glass of water and *maybe* a candle will add to it, if you are so inclined. If you do like to get a little more detailed, you can follow the instructions in the earlier section, but don't feel compelled to twist yourself into knots before you've even begun.

Okay, onto the spreads.

One-Card Reading

[Figure 1]

This is the simplest kind of reading, and can be done in a minute or two. The questioner posits a yes/no query, and the reader cuts the deck and shows the card at the split (see Fig. 1). If it's a red card, the answer is "yes," and a black card means "no." The actual card itself can add a *little* more meaning to the reading, if you care to discuss it with the client, but it won't tell you much. For instance, in the illustration, I've got the Eight of Diamonds. So if the questioner asked something like "Will I meet a new romantic partner soon?" the answer would be "yes," with a slight augmentation indicating that perhaps they will meet their lover due to some office gossip, or that perhaps their new paramour will be a gossip him/herself.

This type of reading is not particularly good for deep questions. The new love question probably is about as profound as it can get with such a cursory effort. However, it's a perfect reading for folks who want to get simple answers to simple questions, or for those "fence-sitting" on a trivial decision. It can also be a nice way to perform a quick daily divination, just to keep yourself in practice.

You could also use a single-card reading as a way to guide your meditative or prayer practice, as the individual card might give you a theme to focus on. These are all just my suggestions, however, and you will likely find your own uses for this spread.

Three-Card Reading

[Figure 2]

This sort of spread is a little fuller, but it is usually linked to a period of time. Make sure to establish that time-frame before doing the reading, asking the cards to show you yesterday/today/tomorrow, tomorrow morning/noon/night, etc. You can be very vague and say past/present/future, but the answers will likely be equally vague. You can also be very specific and say 1pm/2pm/3pm, but that may likewise short-circuit the reading. I generally find morning/noon/night readings are my favorites with this type of spread. In fact, I often do them in the evenings as part of staying in practice. They take about 5-10 minutes and they help me to pay attention to different things throughout the day.

In Fig. 2, you can see a three-card spread displayed. The deck is shuffled, and the top three cards are laid out in a line. Cards are read left to right, with the left-most card being the "oldest" or "earliest" card (the past or the morning, etc.). For the sake of easy explanation, let's say this is a typical morning/noon/night reading. That means you've got:

- Morning – Four of Diamonds: The purse/money bag; No news.
- Noon – Five of Spades: Illness; A corpse.
- Night – Ten of Diamonds: A treasure chest; Sunlight; Joy.

So for this particular reading, the morning would be fairly stagnant, especially financially. As the day progressed, things would feel like they were getting worse, or perhaps some real effort would be needed to "bury" those monetary woes. But by the end of the day, everything's working out, and finances are secure. So perhaps the client will have a money scare (an overdraft charge or something like that) which they spend a good bit of time dealing with, but by the end of the day, it all works out in their favor. Or, it could be that the actual workday (assuming a 9-to-5 schedule) will be awful, going from bad to worse, but that the evening will redeem the day, perhaps by allowing some small luxury time with friends or loved ones.

Five-Card Reading (Full Spread)

[Figure 3]

This is the reading most people want, and the most detailed one I personally do on a regular basis (there's another one where you lay out nearly every card in the deck, but we'll come to that soon). It's called a five-card spread because in its basic completed form, five cards are displayed (as in Fig. 3). I mentioned, though, that this is a misnomer. In fact, you'll actually read *at least* seven cards in this layout, with the potential for several more on top of that.

[Figure 4]   [Figure 5]

I start by "clearing" the deck, which is just a highly ritualized shuffle while I attempt to keep my mind blank in order to "neutralize" the cards for the client. Then, I let the client shuffle the cards while asking and focusing on his or her question. Queries here can be as simple or complex as the subject wants. I know there are folks who do not like others touching their cards, so if you're not comfortable with that, feel free to just hold hands with the client before shuffling the deck yourself. That should at least allow you to get a bit of the client into the cards for the reading. Once the client feels the deck has been shuffled enough (or you feel an urge to finish shuffling, if you do it that way), stop and stack the deck into a single pile. Then the client (or you) will cut the deck (Fig. 4) and put the top half of the pile facing up on the reader's left. The bottom half is flipped over so that the bottom card is face up on the reader's right (Fig. 5). This is the "quick read" of the situation, which will examine internal and external influences on the subject.

For this sample reading, let's assume that the reading is about the client's current relationship/romantic life and where it's going. On the left or internal side is the Eight of Diamonds, and on the right or external side is the Three of Hearts. This breaks down to mean:

- Internal - Eight of Diamonds: Gossip; Idle chatter.
- External – Three of Hearts: A wish granted; A full cup.

So the internal situation seems to be one of pleasant, if light, emotional content. The external component says that the cup is full, and all is well. Basically the cards indicate an extremely happy if rather casual romantic relationship.

The next step is to restack the deck so that the two halves are reversed. In other words, the Eight of Diamonds will now be the bottom card and the Three of Hearts will be the "middle" card. The reader then pulls cards in pairs starting at the top of the deck and going down until he or she reaches the signifier card (the Queen of Hearts for a woman, the King of Hearts for a man). See the process in the following figures:

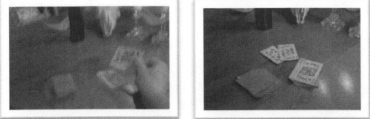

[Figure 6]   [Figure 7]

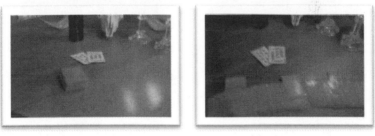

[Figure 8]   [Figure 9]

In Fig. 6 the cards are turned over two by two. In Fig. 7, the signifier (in this case a King of Hearts as I'm reading for myself) has been found, with a Ten of Diamonds behind it. That pair is set aside as it was found (with the ten behind the king, which I'll get to in a minute). The pile of cards overturned to find that pair is put back on top of the unturned pile to make a single deck again (Fig. 8). This group is then splayed or sorted through by the client (or you) and three cards are selected at random (the three "pulled" cards in Fig. 9). These three cards are then placed in a "tree" pattern coming down from the signifier pair

41

in the order they were pulled. You should end up with something looking like this (Fig. 10):

[Figure 10]

This is the basic layout for the reading. The first thing to note is whether the signifier card is on top of or below the companion card. If it is on top of its mate, the companion card indicates internal processes and functions, while the opposite indicates outside influences. In this case, the Ten of Diamonds is behind the signifier card, indicating a great deal of internal happiness and contentment. The rest of the reading has to do with the future/fortune of the subject:

- Companion Card – Ten of Diamonds: A treasure chest; Sunlight; Joy. (internal)
- Signifier Card – King of Hearts: The subject (male)
- Card 1 – Queen of Hearts: Soulmate.
- Card 2 – Two of Diamonds: Birds (as in "a little birdie told me"); Exchange of funds.
- Card 3 – Ace of Clubs: A cave; Solitary contemplation.

First, I note that there are no spades, which indicate a relatively positive reading. Second, the soulmate card appears almost immediately, which is a very good sign in a question about relationships. The reader already knows that the signifier card is surrounded by good things (the interior sunshine and the near future or current soulmate). Next down the list is the birds card. This might mean getting some good news about the soulmate, or possibly even something more significant (think "birds and bees"). It could theoretically mean an exchange of funds for love (an expensive date, or possibly prostitution), but there's not much to support that in the reading otherwise. The third card is a little bit more difficult, as it indicates a need for personal space. So it may indicate that while things are going great now, something is going to take the relationship to the next level (the birds and their associated nesting), and that the subject will feel the need for his own space or time. Conversely, a cave is also the most rudimentary form of home, so it could mean that the subject will be doing his own version of "nesting" soon. All in all, this could mean moving in together, or possibly even starting a family together, sometime in the near future.

The reading can stop here, if the client and/or reader wishes, or cards can be pulled one at a time randomly from the remaining deck.

[Figure 11]

In this "extended" spread, the meanings become vaguer and vaguer as you go further out. Generally speaking, I will only allow 2-3 extra cards during my readings, because after that things just start falling apart. In Fig. 11, you can see I pulled the Six of Clubs. That is the card for "Footprints; A clear trail." This basically just reinforces the current trajectory of the relationship, and for someone who's already started a family or moved in with their significant other, probably just means "stay the course." The current home life is rich and rewarding, and will continue to be so.

[Figure 12]

Just to tie everything up, one more card is pulled (Fig. 12), the Jack of Hearts. This is the card signifying "A baby; A cradle; A young boy." If I weren't the client, I imagine whoever I was reading for would probably get beads of sweat on his neck right about now. All indications are that the natural ending to all this domestic and romantic bliss will be a bouncing baby not too far down the line. It's a tidy ending to a very positive reading, and a good place to stop.

The Fifty-Four Card Reading (Full Deck)

I'll begin by saying this is simply not a version of reading I do often—in fact, hardly ever. It's based on the Lenormand system I referenced in the Overview portion of the book, which uses an extended reading like this to give a complete picture of the questioner's life, influences, opportunities, and so forth. I have already mentioned that I tend to eschew too much ceremony, and this kind of a reading is quite involved, so I don't use it. That being said, it can be incredibly useful, especially if you're attempting to truly uncover a problem and develop detailed solutions. When performing a reading like this, the subject usually does not need to ask a question, as the cards will provided a snapshot of what's going on in his or her life without direction.

The method is sometimes called the "Grand Tableau" method (based on Lenormand readings), meaning the "large table," which is appropriate, as the end result looks very much like a table-top made up of your various cards. You need a broad surface to be able to do this reading well, like a kitchen table or a cleared space on the floor. You will also want to have a good bit of time to devote to the reading, as it can take anywhere from a quarter hour to an hour or more to effectively perform the full deck reading.

In the Lenormand method, you would typically see four rows of nine cards, but as the playing cards are somewhat different, I use six rows of nine cards each. Please note that in order to do this reading effectively (even solely from a mathematical perspective), you **must include two Jokers in your deck.** The Jokers maintain their mystery in the reading, but can also indicate blind spots within the subject's field of view, spiritually and emotionally speaking. As in the Lenormand method, you have key indicator cards which always represent the querying party, which you've probably guessed are the Queen of Hearts for a woman and the King of Hearts for a man. When laying out the deck, the indicator cards will act as a sort of "focal point" for the rest of the other cards in the reading, with varying degrees of influence playing out depending on what falls where.

The simplest way to understand this reading is that the cards in the same **row** as the indicator card represent the past and future of the subject, while the cards in the same **column** as the indicator talk about present influences. Radiating out and away from the subject are increasingly less influential cards, but it is important to note that even the card or cards furthest away from the indicator have significance and shape the overall circumstances of the reading. **There are no unimportant cards in this kind of reading.** All of this will make more sense as we look at an actual example, so let's get to that.

[Figure 13]

You may not be able to see every card clearly here (Fig. 13), so let's look at this arranged a little more systematically. Appropriately, I'll do the Grand Tableau as a table, with the suits indicated by their first letters (H for Hearts, D for Diamonds, etc.).

9H	AS	AD	10C	2H	3D	6C	7S	4H
3S	AH	KS	4D	QS	JOK	2D	3H	5C
7C	KH	JH	4C	2C	AC	5S	6D	9D
10S	8H	3C	QD	8S	10D	KD	JOK	5H
7D	4S	2S	10H	8D	QH	QC	8C	6H
5D	JD	JS	7H	JC	6S	KC	9S	9C

Table: A Grand Tableau reading

Now that we can see just what cards we've got laid out in our table, let's try interpreting them in two different ways: once for a male subject, and once for a female subject.

Looking at the male subject, you can see the third row and second column form the immediate temporal influences:

	AS							
	AH							
7C	KH	JH	4C	2C	AC	5S	6D	9D
	8H							
	4S							
	JD							

At a glance, this reveals a few pieces of information about the person being read:

❖ His past has less bearing on his life than his future
❖ His external and internal influences (the cards directly above and below the subject's card, respectively) are more-or-less balanced

❖ Clubs and Hearts occur most often, indicating a reading centered on love and family, as well as personal callings

The cards directly around his indicator card are the Seven of Clubs in the past, Jack of Hearts in the future, Ace of Hearts as an immediate external influence, and the Eight of Hearts as the immediate internal influence. Since the Seven of Clubs indicates doubts and worries, and the other three cards are Hearts, the emotional life of the subject is clearly at stake here.

So what do we make of these two lines of cards in terms of specific meanings? I would say that an overwhelming sense of isolation, loss, and loneliness (indicated by the Aces of Hearts and Spades hovering over him and the recent past influence of doubt) are coming into conflict with an emotional inability to get into a serious and intimate relationship (the flirtatious Ace of Hearts and the quagmire of the Four of Spades both reveal problems with under- or over-committing). Deep within the subject's emotional being, not surprisingly, is a single person— the youth or girl revealed by the Jack of Diamonds. This could be a current crush which remains dormant or a previous heartbreak of some kind which has been hobbling emotional growth.

Moving along the horizontal axis, the future for the querent is a bit more positive—only one Spade to contend with, and a number of cards indicating success. However, the only Heart is the immediate future presented by the Jack of Hearts. Unless the subject is expecting a new child soon, this signifies that the person is about to have a new phase of life begin, one which promises a lot of opportunity, but not much romance (or any, really). Instead, a strong business proposition seems to be on the table, indicated by the Four and Two of Clubs. The work will also leave the person feeling lonely, though (Ace of Clubs), and likely there will be a major health issue to contend with, based on the Five of Spades. Following this period of struggle, however, things turn around and the streets of gold/peaceful symbolism of the two Diamonds tell the reader that the business is poised for tremendous success as long as the subject sticks with it.

Now that we have the basic axes of the reading, let's expand out and see what sorts of additional meaning we can find, based on the other cards present. For the sake of simplicity, I'm going to pick three cards at various places within the main tableau and look at the cards immediately around them, then relate those back to the querent's card by position and influence. In a grand tableau, you would spend time evaluating all of the cards and their positions, of course, but in the end you would likely have to limit the in-depth discussion to a few select points, or else you'd be interpreting the reading all day.

In this case, let's look a little more closely at the girl portrayed by the Jack of Diamonds, the ill health of the Five of Spades, and the opportunity provided by the Jack of Hearts.

Jack of Diamonds – This card is located in the lowest portion of the vertical axis, and as I indicated above, it is likely either a person towards whom the subject has developed romantic feelings or a former lover still affecting his emotional life. The cluster of cards around the girl are the Five and Seven of Diamonds (laughter and deceit) and the Four, Two, and Jack of Spades (a mire, a separation, and a backstabber or rebel). This is an unfaithful person, someone who has the power to infatuate perhaps, but who will deceive and deride the subject to the point of mockery. Most likely, an old flame or ex-lover with a propensity for emotional—and possibly physical—infidelity. In relation to the subject, the pips are all Diamonds and Spades, cutting implements, which surround the deepest emotional level of his psyche. He has been wounded, and wounded deeply, by this person.

7D	4S	2S
5D	JD	JS

Five of Spades – The illness shown in this card frequently applies to the body, hence its other meaning of 'a corpse.' It is the only Spade in its particular bubble of cards, but the Jokers both could be covering some of the direr element of the subject's life. We'll look at those a bit further in a moment. The remaining cards are a Ten, Two, Six, and King of Diamonds (treasure chest, exchange of funds, streets of gold, and wisdom with money), the Ace of Clubs (cave/solitude), and the Three of Hearts (wish granted/full cup). There's very little negativity here, but looking more closely we can also see something shut away and hidden (treasure chest), isolation (the cave), and overwork (a full cup). The workload the subject faces in getting his business off the ground will likely cause significant emotional distress and possibly depression. The rewards will be great, but the cost will be high. Likewise, the universe is hiding two curveballs in the mix—the Jokers, which sit both above (external) and below (internal) the time axis of the client's future. The cards say that an unexpected external event (top Joker) will have unexpected emotional consequences (bottom Joker). They form a diagonal line through the Five of Spades, which most likely means that they will all be connected, and that the illness could actually be the tool by which the subject can reorder his life to begin reaping the rewards of his business efforts.

JOK	2D	3H
AC	**5S**	6D
10D	KD	JOK

Jack of Hearts – In this case, since the Jack is immediately next to the querent's card, we can put aside any interpretations of the King of Hearts. What remains are the Eight and Ace of Hearts (flirtation and new romance), the Four and Queen of Diamonds (a purse and a wedding/sensuality), the Four and Three of Clubs (a plowed field and a stone wall), and the King of Spades (criminal or male rival). In terms of position, the opportunity provided by the Jack of Hearts is externally shaped by the male rival, and internally facing a blockade of some kinds. The two are likely related, and it is highly likely that by overcoming the male rival will be the impetus to future success, emotionally and in business. We should also note that the cards closest to the subject's card and the Jack are both hearts, which may mean that the rival will be a romantic one—nothing spurs on the desire to succeed like proving one is a better love match than the other guy. The client may not see success long-term in the romance, but the roads opened by the competition for affection might prove incredibly beneficial in other areas.

AH	KS	4D
KH	JH	4C
8H	3C	QD

Now that we've looked at the male of the species, let's see how the cards break down for a woman instead:

					3D			
					JOK			
					AC			
					10D			
7D	4S	2S	10H	8D	QH	QC	8C	6H
					6S			

I'll be a bit briefer in this reading, since you have already seen the mechanics of this reading at work.

The quick glance tells us that the subject has a lot of elements in her past which are affecting her now, and that this reading is less about the future. Likewise, she's got very little emotional subtext to her situation, but a lot of external factors weighing her down.

Her most immediate influences are:
- ❖ Eight of Diamonds – A recent episode of gossip or idle chatter
- ❖ Ten of Diamonds – Happiness and joy coming from her interaction with the outside world
- ❖ Queen of Clubs – A wedding or sensuality in her near future
- ❖ Six of Spades – A feeling of being tempted to do something naughty

She is surrounded by a strong mix of all suits, with Diamonds being the strongest, Spades the next strongest, and both Hearts and Clubs taking on a smaller role. This is someone with a powerful social life, and likely the ability to be both utterly charming and a bit cutting and snarky if the occasion calls for it (based on the sharpness of her two strong suits, plus the multiple 'talking' cards of the Seven of Diamonds/lies, Eight of Diamonds/gossip, and Eight of Clubs/shop talk). Some mystery and loneliness inform her perspective (the Joker and the Ace of Clubs), but those influences lie in her external sphere, so she doesn't feel them deeply. She is likely to grow into a new role due to some upcoming circumstances, which will allow her to demonstrate her ability to be less flippant and more loyal and caring (the good wife of the Queen of Clubs and the loyalty of the Six of Hearts).

Let's pick just one of her axis cards for exploration, then, and see what we find. In this case, the mysterious Joker seems irresistible, and its immediate bubble looks like this:

2H	3D	6C
QS	**JOK**	2D
2C	AC	5S

The Joker shares the mix of suits that marks her axes readings, and is marked by some key factors:

❖ Strong physicality—Two of Hearts (sexuality), Six of Clubs (footprints), Five of Spades (illness/corpse), Two of Clubs (handshake). All of these cards indicate bodily contact or some aspect of the body. The cruel mother/seductress of the Queen of Spades is also physical, although in a less positive way.

- ❖ <u>Exchanges/Gifts</u> – Two of Clubs (handshake/partnership), Two of Hearts (sex, which involves an exchange), Three of Diamonds (gifts), Two of Diamonds (exchange of funds). All of these interchanges relate to the social nature of the subject

So what we glean is a sense that the mysterious influence comes out of a physical gift of some kind, likely one with a strong connection to the body. The Jokers, though, do enjoy being mysterious, so we have to accept that a few hints are the best we can do in interpreting them.

As you can see, the grand tableau reading is quite involved. We could spend a good bit of time relating the location of all the cards to every other card, figuring out why the sexual energy of the Two of Clubs is in a highly external place and removed from the flirtation and emotional bonding found closer to the King of Hearts or why the Nine of Clubs and the Nine of Hearts are at opposite extreme corners of the spread, placing the dark mysterious forest and the little cottage symbols so far apart temporally and in terms of emotional and physical resonance. One of the joys of this type of reading is just how much you can do with the symbols and story revealed through the cards, but on the flip-side, just how much you can do with the symbols and story revealed through the cards can easily become a curse, too. I have only very rarely done this kind of card reading mostly because it requires a copious amount of mental energy to interpret everything once the pieces are all in place. However, if you are the kind of reader who relishes detail, or who enjoys piecing together a good story (see "Telling the Story" later in this book if that's the case), then the grand tableau might be right up your alley.

Sample Readings

Now that you've seen how the different spreads work, it will likely be helpful to see a few different readings in action. Below, I've run through a few different scenarios with the cards in order to give you a chance to see how readings work, and how cards fit together in different ways. There will definitely be some flexibility in meaning, and you might interpret these sample spreads differently, but at the very least you can see my process and thus get inside my head a little bit (mind the clutter and the occasional bat in there).

I'm going to give you three of each of the different types of readings, mostly because I really like the number three, but also because that should offer you a good, broad range of sample readings to study. The exception will be for the Full Deck reading, for which I shall provide one additional example, due to the sheer size and complexity of the spread. If, for some reason, you should one day be reading cards and discover a layout which is exactly the same as one of the samples, please do not take my interpretations as gospel. The question, client, and situation will be different, and must be taken into account to get a real grasp of the cards and the story they are trying to tell.

One Card

One Card Reading: Sample One

Question: "Would I make any money if I opened a book shop?"

Card pulled: Nine of Clubs - Little House; A Cottage; A New Life

Interpretation:

First, we start with the simple "yes/no" side of this reading. We have a black card, which means "no" at the most basic level. But before we run away from this reading—and a life in literary sales—let's just entertain the cards a bit further. True, we have a negative response, but look at the question. It's about making money with a bookstore. Perhaps if it had been phrased "make a living," we might have seen a different outcome. What we do see is the Nine of Clubs, which says that owing a book shop would provide a new life of some kind—which is almost certainly true if the person asking the question comes from a more lucrative field. Likewise, the images of the cottage or little house indicate a more modest lifestyle associated with being a shop owner. The card we pulled is also a Club, the suit of callings and work, so perhaps a change in careers would be rewarding in non-financial ways. What we might take away from this is a reading that says bookstore ownership will never make the questioner rich, but could be a fulfilling job that provides a stable, modest income of some kind.

One Card Reading: Sample Two

Question: "Is my spouse or partner being faithful to me?"

Card pulled: Six of Hearts - A Dog; Loyalty; Stamina

Interpretation:

>The simple answer here is "yes," and it is augmented in a very positive way. Not only do we have a card which tells us the partner is being faithful, we have the reinforcing image of the faithful dog to go with it. In this particular case, the reading does not require much more depth, and the greater risk is in over-interpretation or looking for trouble. If someone is asking a question like this, they likely suspect their relationship is not going well and infidelity is a quick way to lay blame. The cards seem to say that, instead, the questioner should look to other areas where the lovers can improve their connection.

One Card Reading: Sample Three

Question: "Should I be spending more time volunteering?"

Card pulled: King of Clubs – Father; Judge; General

Interpretation:

>Here we have a "no" answer based on card color, but a rather ambiguous value on the card. How does the idea of a father or judge or general play into a question about volunteering? Perhaps the card is signaling that the time spent volunteering would be better used to build a paternal relationship or that some legal entanglements might surface from involvement with a particular volunteer organization. This is the sort of question where intuition plays a large role in interpretation, or conversely, where we must simply accept that a "no" is a "no."

Three Cards

Since the three card reading so generally deals with time, I will provide examples accordingly. The span of the reading will be listed, followed by an interpretation suited to the cards drawn. The answers I give are written as though to a client—my apologies if that is confusing.

Three Card Reading: Sample One

Time period: Yesterday, Today, & Tomorrow

Cards: 1) Ace of Diamonds - A Letter; A Coin
       2) Five of Clubs - Barn; Healthy Body
       3) Jack of Clubs - Sibling; Friend

Interpretation:

> Yesterday a bit of good news came your way, perhaps even an unexpected windfall like the arrival of a rebate check or a card with some money in it. You've held on to the cash—or perhaps even just a piece of joyful information—today, which is very well, storing it up like grain for times of famine. It will be wise to continue to hold back for another day, but in the end your best investment is to spend a bit of your good fortune on a close friend or family member. You might take them out to dinner, or even just meet to talk over coffee and share whatever good news you've received.

Three Card Reading: Sample Two

Time period: This month, next month, and the month to follow

Cards: 1) King of Diamonds - Bank; Civil Trial; Wisdom with
          Money
       2) Four of Clubs - Horse & Cart; A Plowed Field
       3) Ten of Diamonds - Treasure Chest; Sunlight; Joy

Interpretation:

> I would by default assume that the reading was about the financial outlook in the coming months, because the

presence of Diamonds and Clubs in conjunction like this seems to support that. It is also possible, however, that this kind of a reading could relate to legal matters (hence the presence of the civil trial). If we are dealing with money, this indicates making some very wise and prudent decisions in the short term (over the coming month or two) to have them pay off quite well in the final month. In a legal interpretation, I would assume that the process would be slow and gradual, but eventually have an overwhelmingly positive outcome. The two possibilities could be related, of course, if the questioner has an active lawsuit against someone and the end result involves remuneration for damages or something to that effect.

Three Card Reading: Sample Three
Time period: Spring, Summer, and Autumn
Cards: 1) Ace of Spades – Death; Sudden Change
       2) Eight of Hearts – Flirtation; Pillow Talk
       3) Two of Hearts – Lovers; Coupling; Sex
Interpretation:

Someone receiving this reading is either facing some relationship turmoil or has recently passed through it. The Ace of Spades is a pretty clear indicator of a sharp turn away from the current romantic trajectory and into something else, but the following cards indicate a relationship that will develop organically. Perhaps a breakup would be followed by meeting someone new in a few months, which would lead to flirtation and early courtship and result in a much more passionate relationship. It should be noted that these cards don't indicate if the relationship will be particularly fulfilling, but instead simply show forward momentum over a few seasons. Alternatively, since this is so seasonally related, the cards could be saying that there are 'time limits' on how long each phase of the person's romantic life should last—nursing a heartbreak should only take through the Spring, and by Summer it will be time to try again (but serious commitments of any kind, including physical intimacy, should wait until Fall).

Five Cards (Full Spread)

Five Card Reading: Sample One

Client Gender: Female
Question: Would it be wise to purchase the business I have the opportunity to buy, or should I look elsewhere?

Reading
Two-Card Split
Inside Card: Ten of Diamonds – A Treasure Chest; Sunlight; Joy
Outside Card: Ten of Clubs – A Herd or Flock; Clouds

Interpretation
What these two cards say to me is that changing your job is actually one of the best things could happen to you from an emotional standpoint. It's a freeing experience, and it can make you see possibilities where you hadn't before. Some of those possibilities are dreamlike fantasies (represented by the clouds in the Ten of Clubs), but you have the potential to make them something more if you can organize them, sort of in the way a shepherd must herd his sheep. It is fun to dream of owning one's own business, just as it's fun to dream of being a shepherd, but it takes a very disciplined, mindful person to do either thing well, and I think the cards are emphasizing that.

Five-Card Layout
1. King of Clubs – A Father; Judge; A General
2. Queen of Hearts – Indicator card, represents you
3. Joker – Stop Reading; A Mystery (crossed w/ Jack of
      Clubs – A Friend; Sibling)
4. Two of Clubs – A Handshake; Business Partnership
5. Three of Hearts – A Wish Granted; A Full Cup

Interpretation
I have to start by mentioning the Joker. That card can
mean that the reading should just outright stop, but in
some readings I try to be flexible and go with its
alternate possibility: a mystery. Fate is trying to conceal
something from you for a reason. I pulled a "cross-card"
to give me some idea what it might be, but you can't
trust the meaning of the card in this case—it's likely not a
friend or sibling, but instead relates to the suit of clubs
itself. So there is some mystery surrounding your
business prospects, or your life's calling. Perhaps this is
saying that you aren't entirely sure what your calling *is*,
and that figuring that out will be a key to making a good
decision here. As for the rest of the cards, the King of
Clubs lying beneath your indicator card tells me that
you're relying upon your reason and judgment (and
possibly the guidance of an older male figure in your life
like a father or mentor) to help make this decision. That
seems to be a good plan, but again the Joker is waving a
big flag at you to get your attention and say you *must*
figure out whether this business opportunity fits into
your overall life goals first. If it does, then you should
look to form a partnership (perhaps not a business one,
but even a mutual-support one which allows you to get
guidance on business matters when you need it). If you
can manage to perform fulfilling work and get the help
you need, the Three of Hearts says that the end result is

a wish granted or a full cup, which is an excellent result indicating abundant success.

Summary: You do have a great opportunity ahead of you, and in the very near future. It's very likely the same one you've asked about, but you must be sure that you have a passion for and dedication to that business for it to succeed. You will need a little bit of help (the partnership in the Two of Clubs as well as the possible guidance represented by the King of Clubs), but for the most part as long as you remain focused and dedicated, you can be very successful. I want to re-emphasize the need for organization, too, indicated by the flock/herd image on the Ten of Clubs in your two-card reading. I think that being organized will be a key component of the focus required to make this business work. In the end, though, I see a strong indication that you will be happy with your choice, and quite successful.

Five Card Reading: Sample Two

Client Gender: Male
Question: Am I putting my time and energy into the right person?

Reading

Two-Card Split
Inside Card: Jack of Clubs – A Friend; A Sibling
Outside Card: Seven of Clubs – Doubts; Worries

Interpretation
From what I'm seeing here, your internal assessment of the situation reveals a sense of closeness and intimacy with the person, but not exactly a deep and abiding love.

You can relate to the person, but in reality you are both worried that this is not a particularly deep relationship. Most likely you've cultivated an excellent friendship, one that could last a long time, but which may not really be the kind of soul-felt love you expect from a romance.

Five-Card Layout
1. King of Hearts – Signifier Card, represents you
2. Ace of Spades – Death; Sudden Change
3. Three of Hearts – A Wish Granted; A Full Cup
4. Ace of Clubs – A Cave; Solitary Contemplation
5. Seven of Clubs – Doubts; Worries

Interpretation
First of all, don't be scared by the Ace of Spades there. I think that is an inevitable feeling of loss that comes with the hard decision to end a relationship. It's scary, and it's difficult, and it can feel a little like dying for some folks. But it looks like that is what you—and probably your partner—really want: a change, and likely an ending. There are certainly moments of kindness and affection (the "wish granted" being something small and temporary, rather than a fully manifested desire). But there are also intense feelings of isolation, and again the doubts and worries surface in this part of the reading as well. I think the cards may also be saying that where romance is concerned, if you do break up with this person, you'll find you have plenty of folks interested in you, but that perhaps some time to contemplate on your own would be a better use of your time. You had a number of club cards come up, which can indicate a need to focus on your career for the moment, and let romance come another time. It could also be that you really need someone that makes you feel like they are your 'home,' another meaning of the suit of clubs, rather than someone with whom you share a few romantic

inklings, but little depth of affection to sustain the relationship.

Summary: While there may be some potential for connection in the short-term, most likely the person you're pouring your heart into is not going to truly reciprocate your feelings. Instead, you're likely to need to focus on your non-romantic goals, like your career, before romance can really be in your path. This particular romance might result in a long, warm relationship hallmarked by flirtation and some mutual enthusiasm for each other's' company, it does not seem like it's going to end with chapel bells or a love to defy the ages.

Five Card Reading: Sample Three

Client Gender: Male
Question: With recent & new changes to my life, will I be able to shed my negative past, and how will things progress going forward?

Reading

Two-Card Split
Inside Card: Seven of Spades – Tears; Blood; War
Outside Card: Four of Clubs – A Horse & Cart; A
        Plowed Field

Interpretation
You really weren't kidding about those demons haunting your past! You've got some *very* heavy emotional trauma that's been a part of your past, and you've internalized it intensely to the point where you are at war with yourself, and possibly literally shedding blood or tears over your pain. The upside of all this is that it seems like whatever

work you've been doing is paying off. The Four of Clubs shows exactly what you described: something newly turned and prepared for a change. In this case, it's a field which has been plowed and planted, and which is ready to bring forth a harvest, though there will be a bit more work ahead.

Five-Card Layout
1. King of Hearts - Indicator card, represents you
2. Seven of Hearts – Hate; Fear
3. Joker – A Mystery; Stop Reading
   [Crossed with Ace of Hearts – A Kiss; New
   Romance; Feeling Lonely]
4. Six of Hearts – A Dog; Loyalty/Stamina; Long-term
   Relationships
5. Ace of Diamonds – A Letter; A Coin

Interpretation
Once again the pain of the past is immediately present for you. Something has you either extremely hateful or fearful about emotional investment in someone. Normally when I get a Joker in a reading, it's an indication that something needs to remain hidden, or that the reading should stop. The way I read, though, allows a little wiggle room, and so I cross-checked this card with another one, the Ace of Hearts. All that really means is that you should expect a powerful, positive emotional surprise, likely related to relationships and romance, very soon. What follows that surprise is something that will probably be one of the deepest relationships possible, one built on intense loyalty and lifelong friendship as well as romantic love. You should also expect to receive some positive news in the near future which will affirm a major decision you've made or are about to make, and it seems like your transformation

(or "turning over the coin" as it were) will be successful, as indicated by the Ace of Diamonds.

Summary: What you have here is a very good future overpowering a very bad past. There will be a little more hard work (the horse and cart of the Four of Clubs) to overcome the final lingering emotional scars, but then the universe seems to be eager to surprise you with something very nice. Almost all the cards in your reading were red, an indication of positivity, with only the two initial cards symbolizing your immediate circumstances (the Seven of Spades and the Four of Clubs) indicating any negativity. You'll have to be a bit patient, but you will probably be surprised how well things fall into place in the end, and how, once you start making good decisions and having a positive emotional life, you will be reassured of the soundness of your choices. All in all, this is a very happy reading, and actually happier than I expected it to be after the first two cards. Stick to it, commit to the work of cultivating relationships that are healthy while slowly tilling those that have been unpleasant into the soil of your life, and you will find fertile ground for a happy future.

Fifty-four Cards (Full Deck)

Sample

8H	5D	4S	10S	KH	10C	8D	AD	AH
3S	6C	QD	JOK	QS	7C	3C	2C	JH
KS	5H	2S	10D	KC	3D	4D	QH	8C
5S	AS	7S	9D	KD	4H	9S	6S	7D
4C	10H	8S	9C	6D	AC	6H	2H	QC
JOK	JS	JC	7H	5C	2D	9H	JD	3H

I'm going to do a reading based on a woman as the querant for this layout. With that in mind, our axis for this draw is as follows:

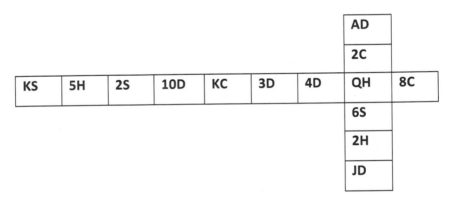

The quick glance at the cards shows us a few broad pieces of information:

❖ This reading is mostly about the past
❖ Very little of the future is revealed
❖ Her internal life is slightly more pressing than her external, but they are mostly balanced

❖ Several male figures are playing crucial roles in her life (two Kings and a Jack within her axis)

Now let's look at some of the meanings coming from the cards in her column and row. I'll break these down by past (to the left of her card), future (to the right of her card), external influences (above her card), and internal influences (below her card).

Past
❖ King of Spades - Criminal, Executioner, Wrath, Male Rival
❖ Five of Hearts - Chapel, Fertility, Bed
❖ Two of Spades - Duel, Separation
❖ Ten of Diamonds - Treasure Chest, Sunlight, Joy
❖ King of Clubs - Bank, Civil Trial, Wisdom with Money
❖ Three of Diamonds - Gifts, Fountain
❖ Four of Diamonds - Purse, No News

Future
❖ Eight of Clubs - Gossip, Idle Chatter

External Influences
❖ Ace of Diamonds - Letter, Coin
❖ Two of Clubs - Handshake, Business Partnership

Internal Influences
❖ Six of Spades - Devil, Temptation, Bad Decisions
❖ Two of Hearts - Lovers, Coupling, Sex
❖ Jack of Diamonds - Good News, Girl

The client's past is a messy affair, or rather, a messy set of affairs. The reader can see the presence of an old flame, possibly a former husband, in the King of Spades. The relationship with him produced something positive, very likely a child (the Five of Hearts signaling fertility, although it could also indicate that the sexual chemistry is what kept them together for so long...more

69

on that in a moment). They ended acrimoniously, which left her feeling tremendously happy, but also a little bottled up (the Ten of Diamonds, with its treasure chest imagery). The separation led to tremendous financial independence, but may also have put her in the path of someone wise and kind (the King of Clubs) who showered her with gifts, but had trouble connecting with her emotionally. Eventually, that led her "treasure chest" to shrink down to the emotional "purse" of the Four of Diamonds.

Looking at her influence lists, money and partnership are guiding her life at the moment. She is stable and secure, but also aches for a little more randomness (the Ace of Diamonds/coin being something you can save or something you can toss in a game of chance). She's feeling tremendous temptation (Six of Spades) to do something naughty (the Two of Hearts). It could be a young man, a young woman, or just someone who makes her feel good (all possible variations on the Jack of Diamonds' meaning). If she does give in, though, her future holds an immediate descent into gossip and chatter.

What she seems to be facing is a love crisis. She has known bad relationship, but now has something stable and good to come home to. However, someone in her life is tempting her to break the bonds of her current relationship and be with someone new. Giving in will only poison the well in her life and lead others to complain about her very openly.

To provide a bit more detail, we'll look at one of the axis cards and its surrounding orbit of signifying cards for some information. Let's find out about this King of Clubs fellow:

JOK	QS	7C
10D	**KC**	3D
9D	KD	4H

Already we know he's got some mysterious qualities (the Joker is somewhat in *his* past due to its location), but we also can tell he's being affected by a similarly bad situation with an ex (the Queen of Spades). Many of his orbit cards are Diamonds, indicating a good deal of financial stability, but his emotional growth is a bit stunted—like her, his heart (the Four of Hearts) is locked away in a trunk or suitcase, much as hers is locked up in that treasure chest. Without being able to really connect past the heartbreaks in their histories, these two are likely to be stuck in a relationship of convenience. They could have passion, potentially, and she certainly needs a sex life (the Two of Diamonds and the Five of Clubs both indicate some highly sexual signs here), but for the moment they are teetering on the brink of a stellar friendship, but nothing more.

In this reading, I would continue to admonish the client to make wise decisions and to realize that her past is really what is governing her future right now. Hopefully seeing a spread like this would help illustrate the problem, but we can't win every battle.

Telling the Story

The Narrative of the Cards

I often hear card readers say that the "cards tell a story." On one level, that is true, for the cards allow a cartomancer to piece together a narrative for his or her client, a tale that will hopefully provide insight and wisdom to the person asking questions of the cards. However, simply saying that three images—or five or fifty-four—can be used to construct a story does not do the cards justice. After all, an imaginative person can take any three images and begin to tie them together with a loose narrative. A person might see a cat, children looking out of a window, and a rainstorm outside and with a few creative pen strokes create something like *The Cat in the Hat*.

Cards, however, are a bit different. They work on a scale that goes above the casual narrative to the level of myth and legend. Books about the deeper symbolic story of the Tarot fill shelves, exploring the Fool's journey through the major arcana and the subtler suit-based stories of the minor arcana. A number of Tarot decks have actively embraced their storytelling quality, including decks based on Arthurian legends, Greco-Roman mythology, Kabbalah, and fairy tales. Playing cards remain relatively untouched in this regard, however, and I think that is perhaps a bit unfair. After all, these cards have rich symbols to draw upon, and the folklore surrounding card decks (see the Appendix for more on card lore) frequently portrays cards as colorful characters in and of themselves. Think but of Lewis Carroll's *Through the Looking Glass* or *Alice's Adventures in Wonderland* with worlds inhabited by card soldiers, thieving knaves, and a ferocious Queen of Hearts and you can understand that a humble pinochle deck can reveal a whole world of fable and story.

In the Tarot decks, the narrative is inherently part of the progressive symbolism of the cards. The Fool sets off on his journey, then moves through different phases of his quest, becoming a Magician, Hermit, Hanged Man, and so forth. Or his story may involve encountering each of these archetypes rather than becoming them. Whatever the case, laying the major arcana out one after the other does the work of telling the tale.

With playing cards, however, each reading provides its own constructed narrative. In essence, each assembly of figural forms (every three card draw or five card spread) provides the raw materials of a new story. Since these raw materials are limited and in most cases related to figures which have mythic or folkloric parallels, however, the stories they tell tend to be ones that already exist. For example, let's look at a simple three card draw:

Card 1 – Queen of Spades – Cruel Mother; Seductress; Jealousy; Female Rival
Card 2 – Nine of Clubs – Reaping; A Forest
Card 3 – Ten of Hearts - Happy Family; A Fire

Now I'm going to play around with those a bit and just emphasize a few elements of each card:
First, we have a **Cruel Mother** (perhaps a wicked stepmother?), who is very **jealous** of her husband's children. She convinces him to send them into a dark **forest** with little or no food. While in the forest, they undergo a struggle with a wicked witch

which ends when they push her into an oven **fire** and reunite with their father, becoming a **Happy Family** once more.

In a highly pared down way, we have the story of "Hansel & Gretel," told over the course of three cards. Of course, a lot is lost in the translation from fully formed fairy tale to three symbolic cards, and this is hardly the only story you could relate to this drawing. The story of "Snow White" would not be too far removed from this set of cards, for example. Let's look at another reading, this time with the Full Spread of five cards:

Card 1 – Six of Spades – Devil; Temptation; Bad Decisions
Card 2 – King of Hearts – Client; Soulmate
Card 3 – Jack of Diamonds – Good News; A Girl
Card 4 – Seven of Spades – Tears; Blood; War
Card 5 – Ten of Spades – Cemetery; A Ruined Church

Again, paring this down, we have someone being horribly **tempted** to make a **bad decision**. The decision seems like **good news** in the short term, perhaps the heart of a pretty **girl** is won. But the couple's pairing results in tragedy: **tears, blood,** and **war**. In the end, their love leaves many dead in the **cemetery**, and their city—here represented by a public gathering place like a **church**—is **ruined**. It's the story of the Trojan War (and likely countless other stories with similar elements). Young Paris is tempted to give a golden apple to Aphrodite after she promises him the love of Helen. Paris abducts the girl as his lover, and triggers a war that lasts ten years and results in the razing of his city to the ground. Again, this might not be the only interpretation of these cards, but hopefully it illustrates the mythic levels at which a simple deck of playing cards can operate.

Personal Note: Fairy Tales & Card Readings

So why go to all the trouble of making these cards relate to one another at all? Why bother to tell the story? After all, the client receiving the reading knows his or her own personal narrative and likely how the symbols fit into the picture, so why go to the extra lengths of tying them to some other tale?

Firstly, I love fairy tales and folklore. I feel that they operate in ways that we only barely understand—providing moral guidance in some cases, helping us struggle through psychological turmoil in others—but largely their impact is something we relegate to diversion and mild edification for children. I embrace fairy tales as a form of mythology featuring human beings as the primary agents of change. While I appreciate a good myth, and sometimes I do relate card readings to mythic tales, too, most of my readings for clients include fairy tale recommendations. I like to relate a card reading to a fairy tale because the cards and the stories can go hand in hand to perform tremendous feats. I think of the fairy tale as a map, showing a landscape full of possibilities for the client, and the cards are the compass and legend which make sense of the map. They highlight the dangers, the opportunities, and the rewards which can come from accepting a personal connection with a specific narrative and attempting to live out that journey a little. When people only receive the partial story through the cards, a full fairy tale can help illuminate other areas of the personal narrative which might have remained hidden in a cards-only reading. For instance, a person getting the five card reading above might read it as simply a bad relationship between themselves and another person, but relating it to the Trojan War might help illustrate that a great many other lives could be altered by pursuing temptation inappropriately.

That is not to say that someone who gets a Queen of Spades, Nine of Clubs, and Ten of Hearts should start trying to find houses made of cookies and candy, nor should they push elderly women into hot kitchen appliances. I simply want to make the case that being thoughtful and aware that we have the potential to act out a narrative in our "real" lives empowers us to be agents of change. We can avoid the wicked witches, or at least be prepared to face them when they appear. We can choose to embrace the task of giving out golden apples, or to at least know afterwards that we should beware of large wooden horses left on our doorsteps. If I were to get the Hansel & Gretel reading, for example, I would likely begin trying to figure out just who my Cruel Mother figure is, and then see if she's setting me up for an opportunity that is too good to be true (like the gingerbread house). I'd be aware that quick thinking and creativity will likely be the best way out of any trouble that does arise (like Hansel's use of the chicken bone to fool the witch). And I'd be thinking of just what sacrifices I may have to make to come away from the situation better off than I was going into it (eliminating the wicked witch/stepmother's influence over me and forming a renewed alliance with trusted friends or colleagues like the children do with their father after their ordeal).

Cards and stories are two tools I use to make sense of the world around me. I share their connection here because I think that it may do someone else some good. I do not believe everyone must relate their card readings to fairy tales or myths, although I do think that their readings will be enhanced by a good knowledge of world folklore (but then, I think everyone's life would be enhanced by such knowledge). Simply remembering that the symbols on the cards can work together in multiple ways and that the cards are more than just pictures and meanings to memorize, will do much to improve any reader's work.

Final Notes

I hope that this guide has been of some use to you. I reiterate that this is my own system, based on several I've encountered and worked with over time. I have found it to be effective, and have had a number of clients say that the results of the readings have been eerily spot-on, or have come true in ways they would not have expected. I tend to believe that the world *wants* to communicate with us, and that cards are simply one method of participating in that communication. For a number of people, tarot works as well or better, and the same is true for runes, dice, bones, dominoes, and many other forms of divination. If you have an affinity for playing cards, however—as I do—I think learning to see what they might be telling you can be intensely rewarding.

Cartomancy is a very personal practice, and will take time to learn. The rewards are great, and learning to read playing cards will yield surprises in unusual places (imagine playing blackjack and getting a very clear message from the spirit world in the middle of the game—it's not an uncommon experience). The most important step in becoming a good reader is practice. That's true of any magical or mystical system (or any new skill, really), so don't get discouraged if you're not great at first. With a little time, patience, and effort, you'll be able to see the world in a deck of cards, and make your own pocketful of devils dance.

Thank you for reading! Blessings and good fortune go with you!

-Cory Thomas Hutcheson

Appendix: The Folklore of Cards

There are a number of excellent examples of cartomancy systems, folklore about the significance of playing cards, and even stories about playing card readers that I have been lucky enough to encounter over the years. Some—such as the "Soldier's Almanack" tale below—have been tremendous fun and insightful to boot. Others, like the extensive "Rhyming Divination" by P.R.S. Foli, have provided a small degree of influence on my system, but have been more or less a curiosity in my collection of cartomantic lore. Whatever the case, the pieces cited below make for interesting reading to anyone fascinated by the weird world of the cards. The small sampling herein provided is a fraction of the lore available to a diligent reader and student of cartomancy. My brief commentaries on each selection are, of course, solely my own opinions and interpretations.

1. ## THE SOLDIER'S ALMANACK, BIBLE AND PRAYER BOOK
   From *The History of Playing Cards with Anecdotes of Their Use in Conjuring, Fortune-Telling and Card-Sharping*
   Edited by Rev. Ed. S. Taylor, B.A.
   Published in London in 1865

Richard Middleton, a soldier, attending divine service, with the rest of the regiment at a church in Glasgow, instead of pulling out a Bible, like his brother soldiers, to find the parson's text, spread a pack of cards before him. This singular behaviour did not long pass unnoticed, both by the clergyman and the sarjeant of the company to which he belonged; the latter in particular requested him to put up the cards, and on his refusal, conducted him after church before the Mayor, to whom he preferred a formal complaint of Richard's indecent behaviour during divine service.

"Well soldier!" said the Mayor, "what excuse have you for this strange scandalous behaviour? If you can make any apology, or assign any reason for it, it's well; if you cannot, assure yourself that I will cause you, without delay, to be severely punished for it."

"Since your honour is so good," replied Richard, "I will inform you, I have been eight days on march, with a bare allowance of sixpence a day, which your honour will allow is hardly sufficient to maintain a man in meat, drink, washing, and other necessaries that consequently he may want, without a Bible, Prayer Book, or any other good book." On saying this, Richard drew out his pack of cards, and presenting one of the aces to the Mayor, continued his address to the magistrate as follows:

"When I see an Ace, may it please your honour, it reminds me that there is only one God; and when I look upon a Two or a Three, the former puts me in mind of the Father and Son, and the latter of the Father, Son, and Holy Ghost. A Four calls for remembrance the Four Evangelists, Matthew, Mark, Luke, and John. A Five, the five wise Virgins who were ordered to trim their lamps; there were ten, indeed, but five, your worship may remember, were wise, and five were foolish. A Six, that in six days God created heaven and earth. A Seven, that on the seventh day he rested from all that he had made. An Eight, of the eight righteous persons preserved from the deluge; Noah, and his wife, with his three sons and their wives. A Nine, of the Nine lepers cleansed by our Saviour; there were ten, but only one returned to offer his tribute of thanks. And a Ten, of the ten commandments that God gave Moses, on Mount Sinai, on the two tablets of stone." He took the Knave and put it aside. "When I see the Queen, it puts me in mind of the Queen of Sheba, who came from the furthermost parts of the world to hear the wisdom of Solomon, for she was as wise a woman as he a man, for she brought fifty boys and fifty girls, all clothed in girls' apparel to shew before King Solomon, for him to test which were boys and which were girls, but he could not until he called for water to wash themselves; the girls washed up to their elbows, and the boys only up to the wrists of their hands, so King Solomon told by that. And when I see the King, it puts me in mind of the great King of Heaven and Earth, which is God Almighty, and likewise his Majesty King George the Fourth, to pray for him."

"Well," said the Mayor, "you have given a good description of all the cards except one, which is lacking."

"Which is that?" said the soldier.

"The Knave," said the Mayor.

"If your honour will not be angry with me," returned Richard, "I can give you the same satisfaction on that as any in the pack?"

"No," said the Mayor.

"Well," returned the soldier, "the greatest knave that I know is the sarjeant who brought me before you."

"I don't know," replied the Mayor, "whether he be the greatest knave or no; but I am sure that he is the greatest fool."

The soldier then continued as follows; "When I count the number of dots in a pack of cards, there are 365, so many days as there are in a year. When I count how many cards are in a pack, I find there are 52, so many weeks are there in a year. When I reckon how many tricks are won by a pack, I find there are 13, so many months are there in a year. So that this pack of cards is both Bible, Almanack, and Prayer Book to me."

The Mayor called his servants, ordered them to entertain the soldier well, gave him a piece of money, and said he was the cleverest fellow he ever heard in his life.

Comments:
This tale, which appears in numerous forms and with many variations, works on two levels. On the one hand, it's a tale of a clever soldier getting out of trouble due to some quick thinking and sharp wits, so impressing his judges that they exonerate him and even reward him for his guile. The story also explores the subtler idea that the cards are far more symbolic than they at first appear, being able to encompass a broad swath of Christian meanings due to numerology, depictions, and legendary associations. The variations, including a 1948 song with strongly patriotic overtones by Tex Ritter, tend to emphasize different meanings for different reasons. Ritter's version, for example, does not cite the deuces as symbolic of "Father and Son," as found in Taylor's record, but instead the division of the Bible into two books: the Old and New Testaments. Frequently the tale is concluded, as Ritter concludes his song, with an affirmation of truth: "I knew that soldier." The multiple functions of the cards—almanac, bible, and prayer book—do not seem to be entirely static, and the numerology has some flexibility. Since there are thirteen cards for each suit, for example, it seems entirely likely a case could be made for lunar associations (since there are thirteen moons in each year, roughly speaking). The story's charm, a humble soldier excusing his meager entertainment

through wit and intelligence, has helped this tale linger for a century and a half in one form or another, and its symbolism can certainly have applications for anyone open-minded enough to appreciate the depth of a deck of cards.

2. A FLORENTINE INCANTATION LEARNED FROM A WITCH

From Chapter III of *Gypsy Sorcery & Fortune-Telling*, by Charles G. Leland.
Published in London in 1891

"It was in 1886 that I learned from a girl in Florence two exorcisms or invocations which she was accustomed to repeat before telling fortunes by cards. This girl, who was of the Tuscan Romagna and who looked Etruscan with a touch of gypsy blood, was a repertory of popular superstitions, especially witch-lore, and a maker and wearer of fetishes, always carrying a small bag full of them. *Bon sang ne peut mentir.* ["Good blood never lies"]

The two formulas were as follows. I omit a portion from each:

Venti cinque carte siete!
Venti cinque diavoli diventerete,
Diventerete, anderete
Nel' corpo, nel' sangue nell' anima,
Nell' sentimenti del corpo;
Del mio amante non posso vivere,
Non passa stare ne bere,
Ne mangiare ne . . .
Ne con uomini ne con donne non
*   passa favellare,*
Finche a la porta di casa mia
Non viene picchiare!

Ye are twenty-five cards.
Become twenty-five devils
Enter into the body, into the blood, into the soul .
Into the feelings of the body
Of my lover, from whom I cannot live.
For I cannot stand (exist), or drink,
Or eat . . .
Nor can I converse with men or women
Till at the door of my house
He shall come to knock.

84

The second incantation was the same, but beginning
with these words:

I put five fingers on the wall,
I conjure five devils,
Five monks and five friars,
That they may enter the body
Into the blood, into the soul, &c."

Comments:

This strange bit of lore comes from the author of famous
the witch-gospel Aradia. I do not know whether the
Florentine woman of whom he speaks is the same as his
informant for other magical lore, but it seems likely to have
derived from at least similar sources. Leland's Florentine
witch performs an act of fetishism with the cards, dubbing
them as living devils, and calling upon them to flee from
their homes in paper and wax and make their way into the
bodies and souls of humans. In this case, Leland provides a
similar incantation which used fingers—another tool in
plain sight—to do the possession work that the cards were to
do in the previous spell. These ensouled cards, with their
attendant devils, provide a rich new source of symbolism,
expanding the idea of the previous piece of lore on the
Soldier's Almanack into something a bit less innocent. The
way Leland's witch addresses them, the cards could easily
be construed as sigils used to invoke specific goetic or
infernal powers. The deck of cards, then, transforms from
an almanac into a grimoire! A portable container of fifty-
four devils ready to serve would seem to be a powerful

magical tool, indeed! Of course, Leland's account may be
exaggerated, with a bit of drama added for intrigue to
expand the already Romantic image of the fortune-teller.
Additionally, the use of twenty-five cards is intriguing—I've
not seen a reading with that number of cards done, nor a
deck with that number of cards in it. The incantations
shared here, with all their diabolical context, are included
for your amusement. If you choose to call devils to work
with you in divination, do so at your own risk.

3. A RHYMING DIVINATION: DIAMONDS-
HEARTS-SPADES-CLUBS
From *Fortune Telling by Cards*, by P.R.S Foli, Chapter
XVII
Published in New York, 1915

THERE are those to whom the more elaborate forms
of fortune-telling by cards may seem a trifle
wearisome, or possibly too intricate to be followed
without a somewhat exhausting effort of attention.
The method which we give in this chapter has the
advantage of being at once simple, diverting, and
varied.

As the rhyming significations concern both sexes, a
great deal of fun can be provided where there is a
party of young people, and who can tell whether the
long arm of coincidence may not use this old-time
practice to bring some loving pair together?

Take a new pack of cards, or at any rate one in which
there are no tell-tale marks on the reverse sides, and
spread them face downwards upon the table. Before
any one draws a card, he or she is requested to close
the eyes, place the right hand on the heart, and say,
"Honi soit qui mal y pense." [This is the Latin motto
of the English Order of the Garter, and translates
roughly as "Shame to him who thinks evil of it."]
The card must then be drawn with the left hand, and
its meaning will be read by the one who holds the
key contained in the verses which we now give.

Diamonds.

Ace. Since that this ace is now your lot,
You will wed one that's fierce and hot;
But if a woman does draw it,
She will wed one with wealth and wit.

Two. Hast thou not drawn the number two?
Thy spouse shall be both just and true.
But if a woman this now have,
Beware a sly and crafty knave!

Three. You that have drawn the number three
Great honour will your fortune be;
But if a female draw the same,
She must beware of fickle shame.

Four. The man that draws the number four
Shall quite forsake his native shore;
But if the same a woman finds,
Both hand and heart in love she joins.

Five. He that draweth the number five,
Where he was born he best will thrive;
But if it's drawn by womankind,
Good luck abroad they sure will find.

Six. He that can catch the number six
Will have cunning and crafty tricks;
But if a woman draw the same,
Twill show that she is free from blame.

Seven. Since that the seven does appear,
Crosses thou hast great cause to fear;
Women, whene'er

88

the same they draw,
Shall not fear crosses more than straw.
Eight. Hast thou then drawn the number eight?
Thou sure wilt be a rascal great;
Females that chance the same to take,
They never will the truth forsake.
Nine. Hast thou turn'd up the merry nine?
Then guineas will thy pocket line;
She that doth draw it to her hand
Will die for love or leave the land.
Ten. O brave! the ten, 'tis very well!
There's none in love shall thee excel.
Only the maid who draws the ten
May wed, but nobody knows when.
King. This noble king of diamonds shows
Thou long shalt live where pleasure flows!
But when a woman draws the king,
Sad, melancholy songs she'll sing.
Queen. Now is the queen of diamonds fair,
She shows thou shalt some office share;
Oh, woman! if it fall to you,
Friends you will have not a few.
Knave. Is now the knave of diamonds come?
Be sure beware the martial drum;
Yet if a woman draw the knave,
She shall much better fortune have.

Hearts.

Ace. He that draws
the ace of hearts
Shall surely be a
man of parts;
And she that
draws it, I profess,
Will have the gift
of idleness.

Two. He who can
draw the deuce
shall be
Endowed with
generosity;
But when a
woman draws the
card,
It doth betide her
cruel hard.

Three. The man
who gets hold of
this trey
Always bound,
always obey;
A woman that
shall draw this sort
Will sure drink
brandy by the
quart.

Four. He that
draws this four
shall make
A faithful love for
conscience' sake;

But if it's drawn by
womenkind,
They will prove
false, and that
you'll find.

Five. Note that this
five of hearts
declares
Thou shalt well
manage great
affairs;
But if it's drawn by
fair women,
They sure will love
all sorts of men.

Six. The six of
hearts surely
foretells
Thou shalt be
where great
honour dwells;
If it falls on the
other side
It then betokens
scorn and pride.

Seven. Now this
old seven, I'll
maintain,
Shows that thou
hast not loved in
vain;
Thou shalt obtain
the golden prize,

But, with the maids, 'tis otherwise.

Eight. Having drawn the number eight,
Shows thou'rt servile, born to wait;
But if a woman draw the same,
She'll mount upon the wings of fame.

Nine. By this long nine be well assured
The lovesick pains must be endured;
But the maid that draws this nine
Soon in wedlock hands shall join.

Ten. This ten it is a lucky cast,
For it doth show the worst is past;
But if the maids the same shall have,
Love will their tender hearts enslave.

King. By this card surely 'twill appear
Thou shalt live long in happy cheer;
And if a woman draw this card,
She shall likewise be high preferred.

Queen. Now by this card it is well known
Thou shalt enjoy still all thine own;
But women, if they draw the same,
Shall sure enjoy a happy name.

Knave. He that doth draw the knave of hearts
Betokens he hath knavish parts;
But if a woman draw the knave,
Of no man shall she be the slave.

Spades.

Ace. Thon that dost draw the ace of spades Shall be sore flouted by the maids; And when it is a damsel's lot, Both love and honour go to pot.

Two. Always this deuce betokens strife, And with a scolding, wicked wife; But if a woman's lot it be, Honour, great love, and dignity.

Three. Thou that art happy in this trey Shalt surely wed a lady gay; Whilst maids who now the same shall take, Join marriage with a poor town rake.

Four. Now this same four betokens you Shall lead a dissipated crew; Maids that do draw the same shall meet With certain joys always complete.

Five. The five of spades gives you to know That you must through some troubles go; But, if a woman, it foretells Her virtue others' far excels.

Six. The six foretells whene'er you wed You'll find your expectations fled; But if a maid the number own She'll wed a man of high renown.

Seven. Now as the seven comes to hand, It does entitle you to land; But maids with this shall wed with

those
That have no
money, friends, or
clothes.
Eight. This eight of
spades foretells
you shall
Wed a young maid
fair, straight, and
tall;
If to a maid the
same shall come,
She weds the
brother of Tom
Thumb.
Nine. Now by this
nine thou art
foretold,
Thou shalt wed
one deaf, lame,
and old.
Females, when
they draw this odd
chance,
Shall of
themselves to
wealth advance.
Ten. 'Tis seen by
this long ten of
spades
That thou shalt
follow many
trades,
And thrive by

none. But women,
they
By this chance
shall not work but
play.
King. By this brave
king observe and
note,
On golden streams
you e'er shall float;
But women, by the
self-same lot,
Shall long enjoy
what they have
got.
Queen. Here is the
queen of spades,
likewise
Thou soon shalt
unto riches rise;
A woman by the
same shall have
What her own
heart doth sorely
crave.
Knave. This is a
knave, pray have a
care
That you fall not
into despair;
Women, who the
same shall choose,
Shall prove great

flats, but that's no   news

Clubs.

Ace. He that doth
draw the ace of
clubs,
From his wife gets
a thousand snubs;
But if maids do it
obtain,
It means that they
shall rule and
reign.
Two. Note that
this deuce doth
signify
That thou a
loyalist shalt die;
The damsels that
the same shall take
Never will their
good friends
forsake.
Three. You that by
chance this trey
have draws
Shall on a
worthless woman
fawn.
A maiden that
shall draw this trey
Shall be the lass
that ne'er says nay.

Four. Now by this
four we plainly see
Four children
shall be born to
thee;
And she that
draws the same
shall wed
Two wealthy
husbands, both
well-bred.
Five. Now by this
five 'tis clear to see
Thy wife will but a
slattern be.
This same five
drawn by virgins,
they
Shall all wed
husbands kind
and gay.
Six. By this six
thou'rt wed, we
know,
To one that over
thee will crow;
Maids that can
draw the same
shall be
Blest with good

husbands, kind
and free.
Seven. Thou that
hast now the seven
drawn
Shall put thy
Sunday clothes in
pawn;
Maids that draw
the same shall
wear
Jewels rich without
compare.
Eight. By this club
eight, tho' Whig
or Tory,
Thy life will prove
a tragic story;
Ye maids that
draw the same, are
born
To hold both fools
and fops in scorn.
Nine. By this brave
nine, upon my
life,
You soon shall
wed a wealthy
wife;
She that shall
draw the same
shall have
One that is both
fool and knave.

Ten. Now for this
number, half a
score,
Shows that thou
wilt be wretched
poor;
Maids that can
draw this number
still
Shall have great
joy and wealth at
will.
King. Here comes
the king of clubs,
and shows
Thou hast some
friends as well as
foes;
Maids that do
draw this court
card shall
Have very few, or
none at all.
Queen. If the
queen of clubs
thou hast,
Thou shalt be with
great honour
graced.
And women, if the
same they find,
Will have things
after their own
mind.

Knave. See how the surly knave appears! Pray take care of both your ears!

Women, whene'er the same they see, Will be what oft they used to be.

Comments:

I include this entire chapter as it is an excellent example of card divination as both a fortune-telling pursuit and as a game played by many people. It puts me in mind of the sadly almost-forgotten work of Dawn Jackson, who housed similar rhymes on her Hedgewytchery site. This particular exercise is reminiscent of "The Wytch of Poor Memory," which influenced me greatly in early cartomancy efforts. Jackson also offered expanded versions of her system, for "wytches" of "middling" and "exceptional" memory. In Foli's "Rhyming Divination," the strong separation by genders provide a commentary on how the cards work differently for men and women: a Seven of Diamonds, for example, seems to imply vexation for men, but has as much effect on a woman as "straw." Learning a poem like this by heart was, at one time, not a very daunting prospect, and I do not think committing it to memory would do any harm. An especially ambitious cartomancer could certainly memorize this verse rendition of meanings or one similar to it without much trouble, should he or she be so inclined.

4. <u>READING CARDS IN KENTUCKY</u>
From *Kentucky Superstitions*, by Daniel and Lindsey
Thomas, 1920.

"In the telling of fortunes, the cards have the
significations shown below:

Hearts.
ace - house or home,
two - kiss.
three - short space of time : 3 hours, 3 days, etc.,
four - pleasant crowd: dining, dance, extreme and
"mushy" social pleasure,
five - marriage,
six - love,
seven – jealousy,
eight - large number of love affairs,
nine - you get your wish,
ten - extreme love pleasures,
king - somewhat gray elderly man.
queen - rather blond woman,
jack - rather blond young man.

Clubs.
ace - introduction,
two - new things in your life,
three - space of time longer than in hearts.
four - crowd: smaller or quieter than in hearts.
five - ring at bell, knock at door, etc.
six - ride in carriage, motor, etc.
seven - journey on water.
eight - business transaction,
nine - sure luck (best in deck),
ten - long journey,

king - elderly rather dark man,
queen - rather dark woman,
jack - rather dark man.

Diamonds.
ace - a letter,
two - very good luck,
three - three pieces of good fortune together,
four - pleasant crowd, less extremely so than in
hearts.
five - diamond ring,
six - money,
seven - conversation,
eight - more money than six.
nine - disappointment,
ten - more money than eight,
king - elderly, very white-haired man.
queen - extremely blond woman,
jack - young blond man.

Spades.
ace - a strange bed.
two - trouble: lie, angry words, etc.
three - long period of time: three years or more,
four - crowd or sorrow: at accident, fire, etc.
five - sickness.
six - funeral, death.
seven - tears.
eight - strong drink, d.t.'s.
nine - disaster. Worst card in deck.
ten - loss (not necessarily extreme like other tens).
king - elderly, extremely dark man.
queen - extremely dark woman,
jack - extremely dark young man.

Fortunes told with cards should involve the use of a new deck."

Comments:

This is another cartomantic system, of course, so why include it here? For one, it's a beautifully straight-forward way of reading. Being able to pull a Queen of Clubs and tell the querant that he or she is going to encounter a "dark woman" demystifies the sometimes vague readings provided by fortune-tellers. Likewise, knowing that pulling an Eight of Diamonds means you'll be getting "more money than six" but less money than ten seems to be a solid answer. The cultural implications of these particular symbols—the Eight of Spades representing delirium tremens, for example—also make them very powerful. These cards resonate not because their figures are highly traditional, but because they incorporate significant local folklore and life. At the same time, elements of these cards do lean on more established symbolism, with the Eight of Hearts and its "large number of love affairs" not being far off from the "pillow talk/flirtation" meaning I assign it. Interestingly, this method insists on the use of a "new deck," which is probably counterintuitive to most readers, who like to build up relationships with their cards. This particular system might not work for everyone, and it's certainly less poetic than some of the versions listed above, but it has a simple, forthright charm of its own.

5. <u>OLD VERONICA & AUNT CAROLINE DYE</u>
From "Hoodoo in America," in the *Journal of American Folklore*, Vol. 44, No. 174 (Oct. - Dec., 1931), pp. 317-417
By Zora Neale Hurston

"Old Veronica was old. No more joys came to her. By day she sat behind the closed shutters of her house and peeped out into the street, watching, watching eternally to see that none of her enemies 'dusted' her steps.

As soon as night fell she would lift her gross body in bed and call to her nephew: 'Come, Pierre, give me my eyes.' Her 'eyes' were a deck of cards. She'd shuffle eagerly - riss, riss, riss! and cut them and spread them. 'See!' she'd cry. 'See that bitch! See 'em! Look at all my enemies working and plotting against me!' She'd keep this up till the early hours of the morning. (New Orleans, La.)"

Hurston's account of Old Veronica reminded me a lot of another powerful black fortune-teller and rootworker from a similar era. Aunt Caroline Dye lived in Newport, Arkansas, during the first part of the twentieth century. She was reputed to be excellent at finding lost things, and eventually gained a good deal of money for her talents. One of her tools was a deck of playing cards, which she shuffled and "read," although the actual cards didn't seem to be particularly meaningful. Instead, they worked to place her in a trance which allowed her to commune with the spirit world and find out what she and her clients needed to know. The following account is a fictionalized version of a meeting with Aunt Caroline based on a recorded incident. I wrote it as part of a larger piece on her which ultimately was published in abbreviated form in the British journal of the occult, *The Cauldron*. This segment was cut to focus the article more on the historical aspects of her life, but I hope it gives some indication what a reading with Aunt Caroline might have been like:

She knew he'd be coming to see her. She also knew he had said not one week ago that he'd never be caught dead going to see that "red-headed devil" as he called her. But she didn't mind names. God had prepared her for that, for names and slights and slanders and all sorts of trials of the Spirit. Her Spirit was strong, and she could weather a few insults just fine. And, after all, here he was, in the den of the red-headed devil herself, on Remmel street where the white folks only came when they needed her help.

No, she didn't mind none, though she shuffled the cards a little slower than usual, watching him squirm in his seat as he cast furtive glances to the doors and windows. She grinned as Jenkins White's knuckles turned pale and pasty where his fingers gripped his knees, as his sweat dripped slowly down his face.

Red-headed devil, she thought. Where do they even come up with this stuff? Her own hair had been white since her youth, another of God's marks on her that she was special.

That she had a gift of the Spirit that she was duty-bound to use for those that came to her. That she must share that gift, free of charge, with any who asked her for help (though she could, of course, accept gratuities and gladly welcomed all denominations, thank you very much). She was no more a red-headed devil than the woman of Endor in the Bible or Moses' sister Miriam, who God had also chosen to deliver messages people didn't want to hear.

Jenkins cleared his throat gruffly, and she brought her attention back to the cards sliding slowly over one another between her long, dark fingers. She had made him wait long enough, she thought. She called out to Spirit, called out so loud it echoed through her head, though Jenkins only heard a little mutter coming out of her mouth. Spirit heard her, came to her, slid inside her old head with all the ease of a dove settling in the eaves of a church. The veil which kept her mortal eyes and her Spirit eyes apart lifted, and she began to lay out the cards.

Two of spades. A duel or separation.

"Someone stole something from you, didn't they? Your pigs, was it?"

"Yes," Jenkins nodded, then through gritted teeth added, "ma'am."

Five of clubs. A healthy body, or a barn. "They're in a barn," she said. She paused, holding her breath as Spirit washed over her. She waited, knew to wait, until she heard almost loud as thunder pealing through the sky, a voice saying "Five Houses."

"What did you say? Five houses?" Jenkins asked, puzzled and frightened and not bothering to hide it anymore. "What does that mean?"

"Five houses down from your own, that's where you'll find them, in a barn," she said, her voice her own again. She turned the last card.

Four of hearts. A suitcase, or a lock. "You go in there, you'll find your hogs. You just open up the lock on their pen and leave it open, they'll come home right quick to you." She put the cards down and looked the frightened white man in the face. "Don't do it tonight. There's folks about watching out. But tomorrow, tomorrow'll be just fine for it. They'll be gone tomorrow, so you go then. Don't say a word about it to nobody 'til after you get them hogs back in your own barn. No need to stir up trouble over this if you get them back safe. Understand?"

Jenkins nodded, stuttered his thanks, rose quickly and toppled his chair. When he went for his hat and coat, he turned back to her, as if remembering something.

"How much..." he started.

"I don't charge," she said. "Though I do accept gifts, if the Spirit moves you."

He looked confused, lost, as though he wanted to be fair with her, especially with her, and so he dug about in his wallet and pulled out a few wadded dollars and crammed them into her hand. He mumbled his goodbyes, strode out the door, and disappeared around the corner before she could even look down.

Fourteen dollars, sweaty and smelling of hog fat, filled her palm. White folks always paid more, she knew that, though she still tut-tutted her tongue as she smoothed the bills out just the same. Walking over to the small vanity by her bedroom, she slid the drawer out, crouched down, and tucked the money into the space beneath the runner bar. It was almost full again, and she'd have to move some of the money soon, she thought. For now, though, she slid the drawer back into place and went off to the kitchen to get a glass of buttermilk.

Comments:
This episode is based upon accounts of Dye's interactions with her customers culled from several sources (The

Encyclopedia of Arkansas History & Culture, and articles by Stephen Koch/Max Brantley and John Quincy Wolf, and accounts taken from Harry M. Hyatt's folklore collection Hoodoo – Conjuration – Witchcraft- Rootwork (1970)). It should not be taken as a literal transcription of any one event in Dye's life, but rather as an example of what an interaction with her might have been like. The card reading performed is not based on any known card reading she ever gave, but rather is my own interpolation based on personal experience with the reading of playing cards for fortune-telling purposes and is intended only as a narrative device, rather than a fact.

Bibliography

1. Anonymous. "The Origin of Playing Cards." _The Journal of American Folklore_, Vol. 8, No. 30 (Jul. - Sep., 1895), pp. 250-251. Published by: American Folklore Society.

2. Bolton, Henry Carrington. "Fortune-Telling in America To-Day." _The Journal of American Folklore_. Vol. 8, No. 31 (Oct. - Dec., 1895), pp. 299-307. Published by: American Folklore Society

3. Concha. "The Curious Curandera." http://www.curiouscurandera.com. October 2010.

4. Craig, Robert D. "'Aunt Caroline' Dye." _Encyclopedia of Arkansas History & Culture_. http://www.encyclopediaofarkansas.net

5. Craven, Lady Elizabeth (as Margravine of Anspach). "Sketches of Society: Memoirs of the Margravine of Anspach," _The London Literary Gazette_, pp. 28-29. James Moyes, Bouverie St, London. 1826.

6. Foli, P.R.S. _Fortune Telling by Cards_. R.P. Fenno & Co.: New York, 1915.

7. Hurston, Zora Neale. "Hoodoo in America," in the _Journal of American Folklore_, Vol. 44, No. 174 (Oct. - Dec., 1931), pp. 317-417.

8. Hyatt, Harry M. _Hoodoo – Conjuration – Witchcraft – Rootwork_. Western Pub., Washington: 1970.

9. Jackson, Dawn R. "For the Witch of Poor Memory." From the now-defunct Hedgewytchery site. Archived

copies available at: http://web.archive.org/web/
20080412025849/www.hedgewytchery.com/
cartomancy.html

10. Koch, Stephen, and Max Brantley. "Aunt Caroline Dye:
    'The Worst Woman in the World?'" *Arkansongs/Arkansas
    Times.* January 2000.

11. Lawrence, Chita. *It's All in the Cards.* Perigree Trade,
    1999. ISBN#0399524940 (Out of Print)

12. Leland, Charles G. *Gypsy Sorcery & Fortune-Telling.* T.
    Fisher Unwin, London: 1891. (accessed via www.sacred-
    texts.com)

13. Parker, Mary Ann. "The Hoo Doo Woman of Arkansas."
    Ozark Mountain Region Website – A division of the
    Arkansas Parks Department.
    (http://www.ozarkmountainregion.com/node/2673).

14. Ritter, Tex. "Deck of Cards." *Tex Ritter: Greatest Hits,*
    CURB: 2011.

15. Taylor, Rev. Ed. S., BA. "The Soldier's Almanack, Bible,
    and Prayer Book." *The History of Playing Cards with
    Anecdotes of Their Use in Conjuring, Fortune-Telling and Card-
    Sharping.* London, 1865.

16. Thomas, Daniel and Lindsey. *Kentucky Superstitions,* 1920.

17. Wolf, John Quincy. "Aunt Caroline Dye: The Gypsy in
    the 'St. Louis Blues.'" *Southern Folklore Quarterly.* Vol. 33,
    1969

18. Yronwode, Catherine. "William Wells Brown."
    Southern Spirits Website (http:// www.southern-
    spirits.com). 2010.

If you liked this book you might enjoy:

New World Witchery
The Search for American Traditional Witchcraft

A blog and podcast which explores folk magic, belief, and
religion in North America (and the rest of the New World).
Join hosts Cory & Laine as they tackle topics like hoodoo,
Vodou, New England witchery, mountain magic, pow-wow &
Braucherei, and other magical systems.
Subjects ranging from American witchcraft history to
contemporary Pagan practice are explored in down-to-earth
discussions and articles, backed by research and scholarship.
You can find out more at:
www.newworldwitchery.com